Do's and Taboos of
Humor
Around the World

This publication is designed to provide accurate and authoritative information in regard to the subject matter covered. It is sold with the understanding that the publisher is not engaged in rendering professional services. If professional advice or other expert assistance is required, the services of a competent professional person should be sought.

Library of Congress Cataloging-in-Publication Data:

Axtell, Roger E.
    Do's and taboos of humor around the world : stories and tips from business and life / Roger E. Axtell.
        p.   cm.
    Illustrated by Mel Casson.
    Includes index.
    ISBN 0-471-25403-7 (pbk. : alk. paper)
    1. American wit and humor.   I. Title.
PN6162.A96   1998
817'.5408—dc21   98-20912

Printed in the United States of America

10 9 8 7 6 5 4 3 2 1

To my father, Albert E. Axtell

(For the story behind this dedication,
read the postscript at the end of this book.)

Contents

Acknowledgments

Arch Ward, the late, great columnist for the *Chicago Tribune*, many years ago wrote a daily sports column called "The Wake of the News." In almost every column, he repeated this well-known two-line motto:

> The Wake depends
> upon its friends.

In those six simple words, Ward voiced the needs of writers throughout the ages.

In compiling this book, I had help from many such friends:

Sally Wecksler, my literary agent, has not only guided me through eight books but deserves total credit for suggesting the content of this one. I never would have thought of a book on humor until one day she remarked, "Oh, it's obvious what you should write about next." And so I did.

Larry Greb served the Johnson Wax Company in international marketing for almost thirty years. In addition, Larry is a great storyteller, and he graciously provided a number of his stories for this book. Larry is president of the Wisconsin World Trade Center in Milwaukee.

John Hough is still making marathon business trips around the world at age eighty-one, and he never fails to send me clippings and excerpts containing amusing incidents from everywhere.

I liked **Mel Casson,** the illustrator for this book, from our first telephone conversation. He was an absolute delight to work with, instantly converting some of my clumsy descriptions into clear, bright, and amusing illustrations.

Tom Miller is senior editor at John Wiley & Sons, New York, and I owe him thanks for making the decision to proceed with this book. He also made numerous helpful suggestions for changes and improvements as the manuscript took shape.

Richard Gesteland is admirable for many reasons, not the least being he has spent thirty years working and traveling all over the world. He is also a masterful consultant on business negotiations across cultures. He resides in Madison, Wisconsin, if you need his help.

Bob Williams (Stevens Point, Wisconsin) and **Ian Kerr** (Greenwich, Connecticut) are two of the most creative and competent public relations practitioners in the country. I have worked in their shadows with high regard and respect for over thirty years. Both provided support and encouragement with this book and many of my endeavors.

Kiki Clark in faraway Ethiopia represents the kind of young person who provides hope for our future. Serving there for two years as part of the Peace Corps, she took the time to describe several amusing incidents when I'm certain her daily surroundings were far from humorous.

One day, I cranked up my courage and telephoned the internationally known columnist and humorist **Art Buchwald.** Nervously, I stammered that I wanted his permission to reproduce his poem titled "The Tourist's Prayer" in my book. "Sure," he said quickly. "Send me the form. I'll sign it and fax it back." Much relieved by his casual, down-to-earth manner, I ventured that several years before I had followed him on a speaking engagement in Vancouver. "Yeah, I remember Vancouver," he said. "And I don't think they've paid me, either." My thanks to a gracious and very funny man.

Harry Franke is a highly respected lawyer in Milwaukee, Wisconsin, but he is also a poet, a perennial master-of-ceremonies, and an all-around talented fellow. He kindly sent me the unique toast reproduced in Chapter 10.

Thank you all.

Introduction

Laughter has no accent.

And no matter where you travel in our world, there is one form of communication that is understood—the smile.

Those two statements are the reason for this book.

So . . . who should read this book? First, anyone who likes to smile . . . or laugh. Second, anyone who has ventured overseas, stumbled, goofed, or made a faux pas and then has had the good sense to laugh at the situation.

This book is a result of thirty-five years of living and traveling abroad and learning that laughter salves almost all wounds. Of course that means *laughter at the right moment.* As you will learn in Chapter 5, Exporting American Humor, inappropriate laughter can be devastating. But for the most part, humor is coveted by almost every culture.

Laughter Also Heals

Scientists tell us that laughter is good for us. It releases endorphins from the pituitary gland that act in a manner not unlike morphine. Laughter can actually dull pain and make us feel good. It is also thought that laughter increases the activity of the cells that attack and kill tumor cells and viruses. You have probably read about the author Norman Cousins, who claimed he fought and overcame a battle with cancer by locking himself

1

in a hotel room to view videos of *The Three Stooges* hour after hour. He maintained that a steady diet of laughter actually caused his disease to go into remission—and there is some scientific basis for that claim. Medical doctors describe laughter as "a miracle drug." It improves our mood while possibly improving our immune system, and it therefore helps make us healthier. "If we took what we now know about laughter and bottled it," said Dr. Lee Berk, a professor of pathology and laboratory medicine at Loma Linda University in California, "it would require FDA approval." The added benefit is that laughter is free and has few harmful side effects.

Laughter comes from positive emotions, and scientists are finding that positive emotions can be curative. In that regard, I have the pleasure of serving on the advisory board of the HealthEmotions Research Institute located in the Department of Psychiatry at the University of Wisconsin (Madison) Medical School. The institute is dedicated to scientifically determining the specific biological connections between emotions and health. The directors of the institute, Drs. Ned Kalin and Richard Davidson, hope to trace the neurological and physiological connections between positive emotions expressed in the brain and the body's various biological systems. While there has been substantial empirical evidence that positive emotions can improve health, no one has yet traced the specific biological links. If the work of the institute is successful, it is entirely possible that in the future we can improve our health, or even help cure illnesses, by activating or strengthening those links through sociopsychological or pharmacological means or a combination of approaches based on the knowledge gained through this research.*

But what about laughter when traveling overseas or when hosting international visitors? How important is laughter when it comes to dealing with new cultures? One answer comes from

---

*If you would like more information about the institute, or wish to help support its work, contact Will Shattuck, HealthEmotions Research Institute, 6001 Research Park Blvd., Madison, WI 53719, (608) 262-6161, e-mail: *shattuck @facstaff.wisc.edu.*

AFS Intercultural Programs. That organization has sent thousands and thousands of American high school boys and girls abroad as exchange students. In the selection process, two main criteria are (1) they are not afraid to make mistakes, and (2) they are able to laugh at themselves.

What This Book Contains

As for the organization of this book, it is laid out by themes—thirteen groupings, situations, or convenient categories, each filled with related anecdotes. As a result, you can read each chapter separately, or in sequence, or you can search for a special topic or theme. Or you can merely pick up the book, open it to any section, and dive in. However, at the end of each chapter you will discover some practical advice pertaining to that category. There's also advice on how to use humor abroad.

For example, in Chapter 1, Words, and Chapter 12, Misunderstandings, you will find numerous tips on how to avoid mishaps in your daily communications, whether you travel abroad on business or as a tourist or student. Similarly, if you are new to cruising, you may find some helpful information in Chapter 7 on ways to avoid embarrassment—correct terminology, tips on tipping, the role of male "escorts," the importance of the cruise director, and so on. These segments—labeled "More Advice"—are located at the conclusion of each chapter.

As I have said, this is a book filled with anecdotes from around the world. A close examination of that word—*anecdotes*—reveals that it means "A short account of some interesting or humorous incident." Synonyms for that word are short story, sketch, narrative, relations, and tales. It's interesting that nowhere in the definition does the word "truth" appear. While the majority of the stories in this book involve actual, true-life happenings, it is likely that some are partly or totally fictional. Humor often has that characteristic. Many of the stories in this book actually happened to me; many were told to me (and sworn to be "true"); and many were told to me with little or no possibility of verification. It's entirely possible that both exaggeration and imagination have entered these pages. If this offends you, I am sorry.

My excuse might be that I was introduced to both storytelling and truth-bending at an early age. As a child, at bedtime, my brother and I would often plead with our father, a veteran of World War I, to tell us some "war stories." I should first explain that one of my father's distinctive physical features was a red birthmark that ran vertically beneath his left eye and along his nose. I believe today it would be called a port-wine mark. Of course, as a child, I hardly noticed it nor wondered why or how it was placed there. One evening as he helped my brother and me to bed, my father relented to our pleas for a story, sat down on the edge of the bed, and related the following tale:

> During World War I in France, we spent much of our time in mud trenches. At times, bullets and bombs were falling all around us. When this happened, we would press our backs into the dirt walls, close our eyes, and pray for the bullets to stop. On one of these occasions, I had closed my eyes tightly when I suddenly heard a bullet strike some piece of metal nearby. The next sensation I had was a burning, stinging feeling right here, under my eye (pointing to the spot immediately beneath his left eye). I didn't realize it at the time, but a bullet had ricocheted across my face. Well, it started to bleed, but I was so frightened I didn't bother to wipe the blood away. I sat there and sat there for what must have been several hours. The blood dried and it must have seeped into my skin, because I've had this red mark ever since.

It was not until many years later that I questioned the truth of that story. But whenever I mentioned it to my father, he would just laugh and say nothing more. (To learn more about my father, Albert, see the Postscript at the end of the book.)

Another apology I offer is that you may have already heard, or read, some of the stories contained in this book. Once again, while many of them are original and relate actual, one-of-a-kind personal incidents, it would be folly to claim that none has not been told (and retold) before by other people in other places.

Many Hands

This book has been wonderfully brightened by the artistry and good humor of Mel Casson, who created the twenty-six warm, whimsical illustrations spaced throughout. As a result, he has succeeded in bringing portions of the text to life. After studying at the Art Students League in New York City, Mel chained himself to a drawing board and a life of cartooning for newspapers, magazines, and national advertising, which he continues to enjoy. He draws the daily and Sunday comic strip, *Redeye,* for King Features Syndicate, and he recently received the prestigious European Phillips Award for his cartoons. He is happily married and lives in Westport, Connecticut, with his wife, Mary Lee.

I have also been blessed with a wife who has a marvelous sense of humor. When we first met, some forty-seven years ago, it was her wonderful laughter, among many qualities, that endeared her to me. She, her late mother, and her two sisters are the type of people who not only laugh easily but also often laugh with red faces and torrents of tears. The same is true of my three wonderful children and their spouses: Mardi and Frank Burns, Kathi and Joe McBride, and Roger and Kim Axtell. Each has an easy and quick sense of humor, and consequently they often serve as test audiences for some story or tall tale. In fact, son-in-law Joe comes from a family of professional humorists. His mother, Mary McBride, is a nationally known speaker and writer of comedy, having written joke material for the likes of Joan Rivers, Rodney Dangerfield, and Phyllis Diller. Mary, assisted by her daughter Veronica, has also authored eight successful humor books and has been extremely helpful to me in my writing and speaking assignments.

I also wish to thank many personal friends. As the winners at the annual motion picture Academy Awards always say, "They know who they are." Only good friends would suffer hearing my stories over and over and over again. In fact, several of them could have ghostwritten this book with great ease.

I am on the after-dinner speaking circuit in the United States and overseas, and so I also wish to thank the dozens and dozens of unknown people in my audiences who have taken the time after my programs to share a story or true adventure involving humor in our global village.

If you are inclined to share your own worldly experiences, I would be flattered to receive them in writing, along with your approval to consider them for a future edition of this book. I obviously cannot guarantee that they will all be used or appear in print. It is said that there are three basic urges in life: eating, sex, and editing . . . and book publishing is rife with editors.

You can send your stories to me at the following address:

Roger E. Axtell, Author
c/o John Wiley & Sons
605 Third Avenue
New York, NY 10158-0012

Thank you!

—Roger E. Axtell
Janesville, Wisconsin

1

Words

I once sent a fax to the manager of our factory in
Peru. In the message I explained that I needed a
head count. I said: "I need to know the number of
people in your factory, the number of people in
your office, broken down by sex, and I need the
information immediately." The manager dutifully
replied: "Here is your head count. Here we have
thirty-five in our factory, ten in the office, and five
in the hospital—none broken down by sex."

Later, in a footnote, he added: "If you must
know, our problem down here is with alcohol."

Words are the common denominator in our communications.
Spend a few years in international travel or international
business, and the impact and the worth of even a single word
becomes startlingly clear.

For example, during World War II, a misunderstanding over
just one word—the verb "to table"—created great debate and
ill will. According to the memoirs of Sir Winston Churchill,
he and his staff were discussing with their American allies
whether they should "table" a certain issue. However, when
Americans "table" an issue, it means they set it aside for consideration at a later time; when the British "table" an issue it

means to place it on the table for *immediate* discussion. "A long and acrimonious argument ensued," Churchill wrote, until finally the two sides discovered their respective cultures had contrasting definitions for the same term.

If you are still curious about the impact of single words, study the word "foreigner." We use it quickly and easily to describe any person from another country. However, check a dictionary and you'll find it means an "alien," or an "outsider," someone on the outside of our comfortable sphere. We also refer to a "foreign smell" as something odd and objectionable; we say that something strange and unfamiliar has a "foreign taste"; and, finally, we may observe that we have—God forbid!—a "foreign object" embedded in our fingertip. "Remove it. Quickly!" we might say to a friend, nurse, or doctor. Also, we regard others as "foreigners," but we never see ourselves that way.

So, here's the test in discipline: Try to eliminate the word "foreigner" from your vocabulary. Instead, use the phrase "international visitor" or "our visitor from (name of country)."

At the end of this chapter, you'll find a segment titled "More Advice," with a series of tips on how to avoid mishaps and misunderstandings over innocent words whether you are traveling for business or pleasure. Meanwhile, the theme here is that communication between different cultures—*even when single words are involved*—can be difficult but also humorous. Following is a series of stories that demonstrate that point.

Confusing—and Funny—Words

In a number of Latin American countries, the word *chili* is used to refer to a certain part of a man's anatomy, probably because of the pendulous shape of a chili pepper. A friend of mine at a large American manufacturing company once invited his distributor from Venezuela to the home offices in the United States for business discussions. The two men worked in the office for much of the day and then took time off to play golf. As it happened, it was a cold and rainy day. After the

"Pretty chilly."

round of golf, they went back to the clubhouse and took a hot shower. As the Venezuelan departed the shower, towel hanging around his neck, another club member walked by and said: "Pretty chilly." The Latin thought for a moment, looked down, and then politely replied, "Thank you."

✝

An American female student at the University of South Carolina was helping to host a group of students visiting from

Australia. At that time in South Carolina, there was a popular dance among the young people called the "shag." Unbeknownst to the American girl, in Australia "to shag" means to have sexual intercourse. At a beach party one night, the girl innocently approached a young Aussie male student and said, "Would you like to shag?" Amazed, the boy replied, "When?" The girl answered, "Now." Unable to believe his ears, the boy stuttered and asked: "Well . . . where??" And, naturally, the girl replied, "Right here, of course." It took quite a few moments of great anxiety before the boy realized she was merely asking him to dance.

☩

Maria Paz traveled from her home in Buenos Aires to a small town in the Midwest as a high school exchange student. One phrase that was used repeatedly by her American friends was "Holy cow!" which was meaningless to her. Furthermore, when she tried to use that phrase she didn't pronounce it quite right. As a result, it came out "Only cow!" (Try saying that. It becomes infectious.) Another word that often baffles our international guests is "awry." I have even heard Americans mispronounce it, saying "AW-ree."

☩

Individual words and how you pronounce them are equally important in other languages, too. Take, for example, the letter "n" in Spanish. When the symbol "~" (called a tilde) appears over the letter "n" in Spanish, it signifies a different sound—the "n" sounds like "nnn-yey." When the tilde does *not* appear, the "n" sound in Spanish is the same as in English. What happens if you use the wrong form? Cross-cultural trainer Tom Newman learned that lesson when visiting Spain. Wishing to tell his Spanish interpreter he would return to Madrid in "one year," he said *un ano* (without the tilde). He should have said *un año* (with the tilde). As a result, what he said was not, "I will return in one year." What he said was, "I will return in one anus."

Here are some other stories about confusing words from Tom Newman:

- In Venezuela, he saw a billboard advertising the classic movie *Grease*. The huge sign announced John Travolta was starring in *Vaselina.*
- In Italy, his friend was struggling to remember and say the word for "onion." He stammered for a while and finally said: "It is the fruit that makes you cry."
- Walking along the Yangtze River in Shanghai, China, a young Chinese man approached him and asked in English: "Do you want me to cut your face?" Happily, he soon discovered that the Chinese man was asking if he wanted him to cut out a silhouette of his facial profile!

✝

The pastor of our local Lutheran church regularly receives messages from members of his congregation whenever they visit Norway. It seems there is a city there named Hell, and his church members who discover this fact delight in writing that they are "visiting Hell, and almost everyone here appears to be Lutheran!" As a postscript, the same pastor asked me, "Did you know that Adam was a Lutheran?" When I questioned how he knew that, he replied, "Only a Lutheran would stand next to a naked woman and eat an apple."

✝

The owner of a firm in Las Vegas, Nevada, that rented recreational vehicles to tourists received a fax from a potential client in Germany. He replied by fax with descriptions of the vehicles available, along with his price list. The owner closed his message with assurances that the German client "would receive the pick of the litter." The German replied, "No thanks, and I am offended that you would rent trashy vehicles." (What the German obviously had done was to refer to his English dictionary for the definition of "litter.")

✝

"Where the hell am I going to get a dog at this time of night?"

Irish comedian Hal Roach explains that some of his country-men take written instructions quite literally. One Irish friend, he explains, while visiting New York City, used the subway system rather late at night. As he exited his train and walked toward the escalator he spotted a sign that read: DOGS MUST BE CARRIED ON THE ESCALATOR. Pausing for a moment, the Irish-man thought to himself: "Where the hell am I going to get a *dog* at this time of night?"

Humorously Idiomatic Words

American idioms cause non–English speakers a great deal of confusion. We sprinkle our conversation with phrases like "It's raining cats and dogs" when, taken literally, that phrase is not only confounding but also impossible. For example, eating dog is a delicacy in many parts of Asia, so you can imagine what someone from that part of the world might envision when hearing "it's raining cats and dogs."

+

A student from Korea told me that American idioms were particularly difficult to comprehend. He said he had studied English for nine years in preparation for attending the University of Illinois at Champaign-Urbana. On his first day at the school, as he was walking on the campus, an American student casually greeted him with the phrase, "Hi! What's the good word?" The Korean boy stopped in his tracks. He thought to himself: "I *don't know* the good word! You would have thought that in nine years of studying English, *someone* would have told me what 'the good word' was!"

Later, trying to solve this puzzle, he decided to turn the tables and ask an American, "What's the good word?" and listen to his reply. So, approaching a fellow student, he repeated, "Hi! What's the good word?" The quick response was, "Oh, not much. How about you?"

+

You should know that other languages have weird-sounding idioms as well. Here are just four of them:

- In Dutch, when saying that something tastes good, the literal translation would be: "It's like an angel peeing on my tongue."
- In France, when you say, literally, "There are many men

standing on that balcony," that also happens to be an idiom meaning "That woman has a big bust."

- In Germany, when you wish to say the equivalent of "Let me pick your brain," you say, literally, "Let me pull some worms from your nose."
- In France, it is bad luck to wish someone "good luck." Instead, you wish them *merde*, which is the word for . . . well, "horse manure." (The explanation is that since "horse manure" is about the worst thing you can encounter, anything else will be better.)

Laughably Confused Words

Why is English so difficult? Just consider these anomalies as pointed out by people like author Richard Lederer and humorist Garrison Keillor:

1. We drive on parkways, and park on driveways.
2. There is neither pine nor apple in pineapple, and no grapes in grapefruit.
3. Why do we have interstate highways in Hawaii?
4. And what about those outdoor billboard signs that say "Learn to Read!" Just who are those signs aimed at?

✝

My instructor in a Berlitz course was a woman from Argentina who married an American and settled in Milwaukee. She said during her early years in the United States, she was bedeviled by the nuances of English pronunciation. She confessed her worst mistake happened at a school PTA meeting. When attendees were polled on what they would bring to a potluck dinner at school, she stood and eagerly offered to bring a chocolate sheet cake, but unfortunately, in front of thirty other parents, she pronounced it "shitcake."

✝

"There are many men standing on that balcony."

S. I. Hayakawa, professor of semantics and former U.S. senator, enjoyed telling this story to illustrate how confusing English can be. It seems one of his international students asked about the meaning of the word "frog." Hayakawa explained, "It's a small green amphibious animal that lives in a pond." Puzzled, the student asked, "Then why did my roommate tell me she had a frog in her throat?"

☩

In somewhat the same vein, travel magazine editor Alan Fredericks was traveling in China when one of his hosts asked for an explanation and description of the word "turkey." Fredericks explained that it was a large bird with huge tail feathers and a distinctive call; Fredericks even imitated the "gobble, gobble" sound of a turkey. He also provided a lengthy explanation of how the turkey became a symbol of Thanksgiving in America, explaining in tandem what Thanksgiving represented. Finally, to demonstrate his full knowledge of turkeys, he related the largely unknown fact that Benjamin Franklin had proposed the turkey become America's national bird instead of the bald eagle. At the end of this admittedly long explanation, Fredericks finally asked, "Why? Why do you ask?" "Well, tell me, then," the Chinese gentleman said softly, "what does it mean when an American says, 'Let's get this show moving, you turkeys.'"

☩

At one point in his career, the dean of Tufts University Law School in Boston spent time in Sudan. After returning to the United States, he received a letter from a Sudanese professor who obviously had intended to write, "Do you still have a soft spot in your heart for Sudan?" Instead the letter read, "Do you still have a soft point in your head . . . ?"

☩

For decades, Danish-born pianist and humorist Victor Borge has poked fun at American English. For example, he asks, "Why is it that [in English] you say you sit *down* in the daytime, but you sit *up* at night?" Borge also tells of going to a U.S. Amtrak railway station to buy a train ticket. "One round-trip ticket, please," he said. The ticket agent asked, "To where, sir?" To which Borge replied, "Why back to here, of course."

American Words vs. British Words

People who travel overseas take comfort when visiting other English-speaking countries such as Great Britain, Ireland, Australia, and so on because there is no language barrier. As we learned earlier from Mr. Churchill's story about the verb "to table," however, that is not exactly the case. There are hundreds, even thousands, of significant differences between British English and American English. In fact, there are large dictionaries now available listing the different word usages between the two. One prominent example occurs when we visit England and rent an automobile. First, as most people know, the British drive on the left side of the road. But that's not the only difference between our two countries. As it happens, *every part* of an automobile seems to have a different name from those we use in the United States. For starters, you don't "rent" a car in England; you *hire* a car. Then, in Britain the hood is called the *bonnet,* the windshield is called the *windscreen,* the dashboard is the *fascia,* the muffler is the *silencer,* the trunk is the *boot,* and on and on.

I once discussed this situation with a businessman from Sri Lanka, who explained, "Yes, in my country we speak British English, so we use many of those same British terms." But then he added, "However, even we have a few variations." When I asked him to mention one, he said, "Well, for example, we don't call the trunk the boot." I asked, "What do you call it?" He replied, "We call it the *dickey.*"

Curious, I asked about the origin of that term, but he didn't know why that particular word had been chosen. So I continued: "Well, how has that caused problems?" He answered, "I was in New York City on a business trip and took a taxi from the airport to my hotel. Naturally, we put my luggage in the dickey. As we approached my hotel, I saw my friends waiting to greet me. Since I wanted to exit the taxi quickly, I shouted to the driver, 'Quick! Quick! Open your dickey! Open your dickey!'"

After a pause, my friend from Sri Lanka sheepishly added, "I won't tell you what that cab driver told me to do."

✝

"Quick! Open your dickey! Open your dickey!"

Here is a list of common, innocent American words and terms that will cause a British person to blush with embarrassment.

stuffed	fanny
randy	buggered
sharp	vest
napkins	on the job

Now here is how a British person defines each of those terms:

stuffed: Vulgar slang for "having sex with a woman"; or if used as *Get stuffed!* it means "go to hell!" Another bit of British slang meaning "to engage in sex" is to *bonk*.

fanny: In England, this word does not refer to a person's derriere but instead to a female's genitalia. Similarly, a *willy* is, for an Englishman, his penis. (Which makes one wonder what reaction the British had over the American stage play and movie *Fanny* and the more recent movie *Free Willy*.)

randy: This is not the familiar form of the name Randolph; in England, it is synonymous with the American word "horny."

buggered: An American might say, "I'll be buggered," meaning confused or confounded; or we might refer to a cute child or animal as "a cute little bugger." But in England, to be *buggered* is to commit sodomy. In English business lingo, the *buggeration factor* is akin to Murphy's Law (i.e., "What can go wrong usually does").

sharp: If an American describes a colleague as "sharp," it is a compliment, meaning the person is quick, intelligent, and able; but in England, it means the person is devious and unprincipled.

vest: What an American calls a "vest" is known as a *waistcoat* to an English person; a *vest* in England is an undershirt, so Americans should be wary of admiring an Englishman's vest.

napkins: In England, *napkins* are "diapers," also referred to as *nappies;* a table napkin in England is called a *serviette.*

on the job: In England, this is a slang expression for "having sex," which explains why one British gentleman expressed delight when an American acquaintance casually mentioned that his father "was eighty years old when he died on the job."

In a turn of the tables, the following is a list of British words that will fall oddly on American ears but are as innocent as a baby's smile in England:

pecker	bangers	to knock up
rubber	pissed	scheme
cheap	homely	to bomb
vet	tinkle	spotted dick

Here are the definitions for those words when used in Great Britain:

Pecker refers to the chin; so don't be surprised if a Britisher says to you, in an attempt to perk up your spirits, "Keep your pecker up."

Bangers are sausages in Great Britain, which means you might hear a pub patron order "a beer and a banger, please."

To knock up can be used with complete impunity in several situations in England. It can mean "to wake me up" on the telephone; or, in the game of tennis, it can mean rallying the ball back and forth in practice before starting a game. (Note: On my first trip to England, I was invited to play tennis with a charming young lass who coolly inquired, "Would you like to knock up first?")

Rubber is the word for "eraser"; therefore, you can understand why a Florida PR executive was once shocked on hearing an English architect friend cry out, "Who nicked my rubber? It was my favorite rubber. I had it for over three years!" Later, the PR executive deciphered his friend's complaint to mean "Who stole my eraser?"

Pissed is not an expression of anger, as it is in the United States; in England, it usually means someone is very drunk.

Scheme, for most Americans, is a negative word, because we consider a scheme something that is a bit sly and slick; in England, however, it is just a synonym for the word "plan."

Cheap, for Americans, connotes something of poor quality; in England, however, it is used more often to refer to something inexpensive, as in a *cheap day ticket* on the railroad.

Homely does not mean unattractive in England; rather, it is just the opposite—a person in England who is homely is "homelike," meaning a warm and comfortable person.

To bomb in the United States is decidedly bad. A show that "bombs on Broadway" is a failure. But in England, something that "went like a bomb" is a great success.

Vet does not refer to a veterinarian; instead, it is used as a verb and means "to thoroughly check something over," as in the phrase "Let me vet your proposal before we send it."

Tinkle is used as in the statement "Give me a tinkle," which means to phone someone. The British would also say, "I will *ring* you tomorrow."

Spotted dick is a pudding, and the "spots" are ordinary raisins; you'll find this unique dessert listed frequently on English menus.

Wrong Words

The English language has many quirks, twists, and surprises. One of the best known is an oxymoron, meaning a pair of words that actually contradict each other. Common examples are jumbo shrimp, bluegrass, plastic glasses, evaporated milk, and the reference to a golf club as a "metal wood." Also, in

Washington, D.C., a well-known U.S. senator once referred to the Iran-Contra scandal as a "transparent cover-up." That's an oxymoron of the first order.

If that isn't bad enough, even though there are about 750,000 words in the English language, we have a social situation in North America for which we do not have an agreed-upon label. That occurs when your son or daughter is living with someone of the opposite sex and they are not married—what is the proper way to introduce that person? Terms like "friend," "sweetheart," "roommate," and "partner" are sometimes heard, but they all have well-established separate meanings. One phrase that has gained modest popularity in the media is "significant other," but in everyday conversation, that term has still not gained widespread acceptance. In the U.S. census of 1990, the government tried to solve this problem by labeling such people as "POSSLQs," meaning "persons of the opposite sex sharing living quarters." That hasn't been adopted, either. How many times have you heard someone introduced as "my POSSLQ"?

On two occasions, I have challenged audiences to solve this problem. In one instance, a person responded that he used the phrase "err ah." When I asked him to explain, he said his reply was, "I say, 'I'd like you to meet my errrr . . . ahhhh.'"

On the other occasion, I said to a group of business executives and their spouses, "This is a creative group. Let's try to solve this problem. Let's decide what is a good term to use when introducing the person living with your son or daughter if they are not married. What should we call him or her?" A woman in the back row jumped up, clearly agitated, and said, "That's easy! I call him 'that son-of-a-bitch.'"

+

The wrong words can also create serious consequences. During business negotiations with a Japanese businessman, I once said, "Well, our thinking is in parallel." He went away and I didn't hear from him for weeks and weeks. Finally, I phoned him and said, "What has happened? I thought our discussions were moving along nicely." He replied, "I did, too. But you used a word that I didn't quite understand so I looked it up in the dictionary. The word 'parallel' means 'two lines that never touch.'"

He thought I was saying, "Our thinking is separate, apart . . . and will never touch."

Right Words

The worst offense Americans commonly commit about their neighbors to the north, Canadians, is to stereotype them as "just like us." Canadians have a very proud heritage—many can speak two languages fluently—plus they are proud of their diverse ethnic makeup. Consequently, from Canada come these definitions:

1. Americans are said to be "benevolently ignorant" about Canadians. Meanwhile, Canadians are said to be "malevolently well informed" about Americans.
2. One definition of a Canadian is "an unarmed American with health insurance."

Sir Winston Churchill was apparently one of those who could fashion just the right retort, or the perfect rejoinder. Here are just two examples:

- When Lady Astor said to him, "If you were my husband, I'd put poison in your coffee," Churchill replied, "If you were my wife, I'd drink it."
- George Bernard Shaw invited Churchill to the opening-night performance of his play *Saint Joan*. At that time, Churchill had just lost a parliamentary election and, twisting the knife, Shaw sent two tickets with the message "One [ticket] for yourself and one for a friend—if you have one." In response, Churchill wrote that he could not

attend but asked if he could have tickets for the second night's performance—"if there is one."

+

Americans are notoriously ethnocentric, especially about their language. A standard joke among worldly travelers is to ask this series of questions: "What do you call a person who speaks three languages?" Answer: "Trilingual." "What do you call a person who speaks two languages?" Answer: "Bilingual." What do you call a person who speaks only one language?" Answer: "An American."

H. L. Mencken, the American editor, critic, satirist, and author of works on the American language, cleverly summed up the American narrow attitude toward learning other languages like this: "If English was good enough for Jesus Christ, it's good enough for me."

How and When to Use Humor Abroad

We Americans tend to rely on single words to evoke humor: the surprise ending, the exaggeration, the last-second twist, the shocker. Other languages do the same. But as we have learned here, while the wrong word in the wrong place at the wrong time can be funny, it can also lead to damaging misunderstandings. So, as you travel abroad, in your early relationships with other nationalities, *it is best to tread lightly when relying on individual words or phrases to generate humor.* As you become better acquainted with each other you will discover—slowly—what makes each of you laugh. Let those discoveries be your guide.

More Advice

By this point, I hope it's obvious that single words (and phrases) can be like those old-fashioned exploding cigars: when they blow up, everyone around you laughs, and you end up with soot all over your face.

Following are a half-dozen tips for communicating more effectively in American English when traveling the globe or when hosting international visitors.

Tip #1 Speak and write using simple vocabulary. Avoid all of the following:

- idioms ("flatter than a pancake.")
- slang ("We don't want any hanky-panky with this business deal.")
- euphemisms ("I need to visit the little boys' room.")
- sports terminology ("This project will be a slam dunk.")
- acronyms ("We need an answer ASAP.")
- jargon ("My modem is 33 BAUD, but with fiber I'll be up to 56.")

Tip #2 Speak slowly and distinctly. Among international travel savants, it is said you can determine who the experienced professionals are by the slow pace of their speech.

Tip #3 Enunciate clearly. This means avoiding those words and contractions we Americans seem to slur into one clipped word:

gonna	comin'
wanna	goin'
wouldja	whatcha
oughta	saying "ya" instead of "you"
shoudda	saying "em" instead of "them"
	saying "yeah" instead of "yes"

Tip #4 If, in your conversations or discussions, you sense that something has suddenly gone sour—a stiffening of the body, a grimace of the face, or a general coolness in manner—stop and reflect on, or even inquire, if perhaps you used a word or phrase that caused confusion.

Tip #5 As you'll read in Chapter 5, Exporting American Humor, avoid any play on words, double entendres, complicated metaphors, or unusual analogies.

Tip #6 Be sensitive about accents and pronunciation of certain words. For example, some international acquaintances may have difficulty understanding Americans with southern accents. Or they may have learned British English, where many words are pronounced differently from American English. Examples: SHED-ule for schedule, la-BOOR-itory for laboratory, PAHS for pass, PAH-don for pardon, and so on.

✝

For more tips on avoiding confusion, refer to the section "More Advice" in Chapter 12, Misunderstandings.

2

The "S" Word—SEX

An American businessman was paying his first visit to Rio de Janeiro, Brazil. One evening he went to the cocktail lounge at his hotel and took a seat at the bar. Within a few moments, an attractive young lady with a short skirt and heavy makeup sat next to him. He turned to her and asked, "Do you speak English?" "Yes," she replied. "How much?" he asked.

"Fifty dollars," she replied.

Attitudes toward sex vary widely from country to country. A safe generalization, however, is that the United States is considered on the right-of-center, conservative side. For example, prostitution is freely accepted in places like Germany, the Netherlands, Denmark, the Philippines, Thailand, Japan, Korea, and Hong Kong. Pornography has been open and legally available in the Scandinavian countries for decades, long before it was liberalized in the United States. At the opposite end of the spectrum are countries like Afghanistan and other devout Muslim countries where women wear veils and are forbidden to reveal full facial features, ankles, or even bare arms.

As American businesspeople travel among the more liberal

cultures they are surprised, embarrassed, and even shocked by the amount of sexual openness available in many major cities. Most are stunned to find that as a common sign of hospitality, their international business contacts may offer to provide sexual partners. Similarly, some international visitors to the United States occasionally shock their American business hosts by hinting that they would like to be provided with various sexual pleasures.

In summary, experienced American travelers usually arrive at one basic conclusion about the "S" word: We Americans are considered to be more puritanical than promiscuous.

The following stories help demonstrate that premise.

Amusing Traditions

In 1978, I was assigned to manage my company's Latin American operations, consisting of five factories and thirty-five distributor markets. In Argentina, I remember reviewing the financial books and pausing at the account for salesmen's compensation. Under travel expenses I noted an unfamiliar heading, which I translated as "biological necessities." Confused, I asked the general manager of the company what that meant. He stuttered and stammered for a moment and then explained that it was the custom in his country to allow their traveling salesmen to include the expense of hiring a woman to sleep with, "but only after one week away from home," he quickly added. "We are, after all, a very moral country, so we consider it a 'biological necessity.'"

✝

Two engineers from a midwestern auto manufacturer were sent to the firm's factory in northern Mexico on a work project. Since it was their first visit, they were unacquainted with temperatures in Mexico at that time of the year—the month of March—but they assumed the weather would be warm. Consequently they wore summer-weight clothes. When they arrived at their hotel, they found conditions much colder than expected. To compound the problem, there was no central heating in their hotel and they could not find any warm blankets in their rooms. That night, one of the men was so cold he wore his suit to bed. The next morning, using their high school Spanish, they complained to the desk clerk, who assured the men he would take care of the problem. When the two returned to the hotel that evening for dinner, two attractive young women wearing tight skirts approached their table and sat down. In halting English they explained that the hotel clerk had sent them: "We are here to make sure you no get cold again tonight."

✝

A businessman from North Carolina was paying his first visit to Japan. One evening he phoned home to relate to his wife some of the unusual customs and traditions he was encountering. "One of the common practices here is nude communal

"The hotel has run out of blankets. The manager sent us to make sure you no get cold again tonight."

bathing," he explained. "I really think I ought to try some of these traditions, don't you?" he asked. "Yes," she replied, "but if you are going to bathe with nude women, there is another tradition in Japan that you might consider. It's called *hari-kari.*"

✝

The well-known and respected cross-cultural trainer James Bostain tells this true story about one of the unusual customs Americans may encounter in Japan. It seems that an American businessman had spent weeks in complex negotiations with a firm in Tokyo; finally, when the business deal was completed, he and his counterpart shook hands to seal the agreement. The Japanese executive then announced, "Fine! Now, it is our tradition to celebrate, so we will all go to the local brothel." Stunned, the American stammered, "But . . . but . . . but what about your wife?" Not understanding at first, but finally comprehending the question, the Japanese smiled, waved a hand, and replied, "Oh, no. She won't want to come with us."

✝

If you take a tour around Manila in the Philippines, it is likely your tour guide will announce that many of the local residents take great pride in "how well our red-light district is organized." Then your guide may very well give an explanation like this one: The red-light district in Manila is located in one long series of city blocks. It begins with the discos ("where, if you feel you want a companion, you can meet one"), followed by the restaurants ("where, if you are hungry, you can take your companion to dinner"). These are then followed by the hotels ("where, if you wish, you can take your companion for sex"). Next to the hotels are the medical clinics ("where, if you are worried, you can receive medications"). Finally, she explains, there is a long row of churches ("where, if you are feeling guilty, you can confess your sins").

✝

In South Korea, it is customary to provide royal treatment for business guests, especially if they are buyers. Accordingly, one of the large multinational companies there maintains an elaborate guest facility for its business visitors. The buildings contain several dining rooms, bars, recreation rooms, and, of course, numerous hotel-type guest rooms. A relative of mine was purchasing equipment from this particular company, so as a valued customer, each time he visited South Korea he received this traditional blue-ribbon treatment. He reported that the dinners were always elaborate, wine flowed freely, and each male guest was assigned a beautiful young waitress/companion. The food was plentiful, drinking was constant, and singing and dancing were required.

At the end of the evening, my relative thanked his hosts and retired to his room . . . only to find his female dinner companion waiting there for him. She explained she was there to provide him with "pleasure." Uncomfortable at being put in this position, my relative explained that he was happily married and that this situation was not common in the United States. He tried to thank the girl and usher her to the door. At that point, the girl closed the door, broke into tears, and explained that if she was observed leaving his room at such an early hour, she would be reprimanded and a black mark would appear on her employment records. She begged the man to allow her to remain, saying she would sleep quietly on the couch. After considering this proposal, the man relented, went to bed, and later that night awoke to observe that the young woman had quietly disappeared.

At least that was the story he told us.

Strange Sex

On my first trip to Amsterdam, my business host took me on a nighttime tour of the city. He explained that prostitution was decriminalized and regulated in Amsterdam, with the minimum age of eighteen required to work in the sex industry. Brothels are tolerated as long as they follow health and fire codes. Therefore, one of the most popular tourist sights in Amsterdam is the unusual but busy red-light district, located in the center of the city near the railway terminal. Printed guidebooks are available listing the various licensed bordellos, along with prices for the services offered in each. The district consists of one long street lined with town houses, each building fronted with large bay windows. The prostitutes sit brazenly behind the windows, illuminated by special lighting and literally displaying their wares while waiting for customers. When a patron ascends the steps and enters the building, the woman draws the drapes as if to signal "busy."

"Is this district considered safe?" I asked my host. "I mean, is it safe for casual visitors like us to be walking around like this?" He quickly reassured me: "Oh, yes, yes. Completely safe." Then, after a pause, he added: "Well, on the other hand, they recently found a man's body stuffed into a trunk. He had been completely dismembered." After another pause, he added, "They have ruled out suicide."

✝

Flying back from Singapore in the late 1980s, I found myself seated in the upper lounge of a Boeing 747 chatting with an American oil company executive who spent six months each year working in Southeast Asia and was now returning to America. After a couple of cocktails, he finally shook his head slightly, smiled, and said, "I had an experience this trip that I'm still laughing about." With that, plus a third drink, he told me the following tale that he swore was the absolute truth: It seems during this last stay in Singapore, he had established a romantic relationship with a beautiful Singaporean woman. One afternoon, while walking through the lobby of his hotel, he was surprised to spot an old college chum. Since they had not seen one another for more than a decade, they immediately sat down and brought each other up-to-date on personal developments. Finally, the oil executive said, "Look—my girlfriend and I are going out for dinner and dancing tonight. Why don't you join us? Maybe my girlfriend can find you a date." The other man agreed. The oilman explained the challenge to his girlfriend, who at first protested that it would be difficult given such short notice. But then, glancing around the hotel lobby, she noticed a very beautiful local girl she had seen socially and who might be both approachable and available. She went to the girl, sat down and explained the situation, and, after further discussion and consideration, found that the other woman was both free that evening and agreeable.

The foursome departed for a fine restaurant, followed by a visit to a lively local disco. Everyone seemed to be thoroughly enjoying each other's company when the oilman noticed that his girlfriend had become somewhat quiet. "What's wrong? Is something wrong?" he inquired softly. The girlfriend leaned toward him and whispered, "I think . . . I'm not absolutely certain yet . . . but I think . . . maybe . . . your friend's date is . . . is *not* a woman."

Stunned, the oil executive agonized over what to do or what to say. "They were having such a good time together," he explained to me, "I didn't want to abruptly spoil the party . . . so I just decided to do nothing."

After an hour or two, it was time to depart. Arm in arm and laughing, the school chum and his date hailed a taxi and said their good-byes. The next morning, the two men met for breakfast. Casually and cautiously, the oilman finally asked his friend, "How'd it go last night?" He said his friend smiled rather enigmatically and simply replied, "Uh . . . very interesting."

"I still haven't learned exactly what happened," the oil executive told me. "I'm dying to know . . . but I'm afraid to ask!"

✝

News item from a newspaper in Thailand: In the city of Nakhon Ratchasima, a woman, apparently upset that her husband had taken a minor wife, drugged the man, cut off his penis, and attached it to a bunch of balloons. She released the balloons into the sky early Sunday morning, police reported. She did that so he would be unable to have his severed penis reattached. According to police, the man said he suspected something irregular might happen when his wife returned home that morning, saying, "Today, there will certainly be an elephant fair," which in the Thai language means, "something big will happen." Furthermore, seemingly resigned to the fact he would never be reunited with his lost organ, the husband declined to press charges against his wife.

(*Comment: Well . . . you win some, you lose some.*)

✝

As I said earlier, prostitution is legal in Denmark—*but not if it is a full-time job!* To be legal, it must be a part-time, second job. You might say that in Denmark, the law requires that redlighting must also be moonlighting.

Humorously Misunderstood Sex

Norine Dresser, in her charming book *Multicultural Manners* (Wiley, 1996), describes her experiences as a teacher of English as a second language in Los Angeles where cultural diversity is probably at the highest level in the United States. On one occasion, she was asked to substitute for another teacher who was ill. On the appointed evening, she entered the classroom, introduced herself, and asked what the class had been studying recently. "Idioms," several replied. "OK," Norine said. "Do any of you have any examples of idioms, or problems with idioms, that you don't understand?" An attractive young Asian woman raised her hand and said, "I have one phrase I don't understand. What does it mean when a man approaches you and says, 'Can I feel you up?'" Norine was momentarily stunned: "Oh, my God!" she thought. "My first question and it involves the American fascination with women's breasts." Norine played for time by asking: "Where and how was this idiom used?" The young woman explained: "Well, every time I go to my local gas station, this young man comes over to my car and says, 'Can I feel you up?'"

✝

"Can I feel you up?"

Kiki Clark is a delightful young lady who, at this writing, is donating two years of her life to a Peace Corps assignment in Ethiopia. When I wrote her asking for some examples of amusing incidents in her unique life, she provided these anecdotes:

- One day when she was teaching English she was rolling her Rs, as children do when imitating the sound of a machine gun. She found out later that in Ethiopia that sound is used to indicate the noise for passing gas.
- She once entered a small shop and thought she was asking in Arabic to buy eggs, but instead she was saying the word for "penis."

- She was unconsciously making a clicking noise with her tongue. Later she found out this very same noise is done to male children by their fathers to erect their penises.

Finally, one day Kiki was on a long country walk with a friend and noticed a boy riding on a donkey. "It looked like fun," she wrote, "and so I asked if I could have a ride. When I jumped on top, the boy and my friends all doubled over in laughter. They laughed even harder when I jokingly started singing a Christmas hymn because I was feeling a bit like the Virgin Mary. Later I found out that the only time women in Ethiopia ride donkeys is when they have been rejected by their new husbands for not being a virgin."

✝

Steve works for a company in the forging industry. His company set up operations in Ireland, and Steve is required to travel there frequently. One evening, after work, Steve and several of the company's office personnel—including several young women—visited a local pub for a few drinks and a light supper. As they were departing the pub after the meal, Steve turned to one of the young women and casually asked: "Would you like a ride?" She looked startled, then offended, turned, and walked away. Later, Steve learned that in that part of Ireland, the phrase "Would you like a ride?" is tantamount to asking, "Would you like to have sex?"

✝

In Britain some of my English friends told me they could tell a great deal about a man's personality by the way he grows bald. If a man grows bald in front, at the hairline, it means, "He is a thinker." However, if his balding pattern begins at the back of the head, "He is sexy." And what if he grows bald in both places at once? "That means he thinks about sex too much."

†

George and Stella moved from Wisconsin to England for a one-year university sabbatical in London. With them was Mary, their infant daughter. Naturally, the couple was nervous about traveling so far from home with their tiny baby. Arriving in London, George found a comfortable flat to rent and, even though still apprehensive, the young family tried to begin their new lifestyle. At night, Stella kept Mary in a crib alongside the couple's bed. In this way, she could reach out easily, bring her into bed, and sit up and nurse her. After a week or so, Stella found that she was falling off to sleep while Mary was still suckling. Stella would wake with a jerk, realize she still held Mary in her arms, and return her to her crib. Stella developed a nagging fear that she would drift off to sleep, fail to put Mary back in her crib, and roll over and smother her.

On one of these occasions, Stella nursed Mary and fell half-asleep but returned the baby to her crib. At this point, George picks up the story: "I was awakened from a deep sleep by Stella shouting: 'George! George! Wake up! Wake up! We've smothered Mary! We've smothered her! I *know* we have! She's down here—right here!—right between us! I know! I know! . . . because *I've got her by the arm!*' I woke up instantly, of course. My immediate thought was I had to save my baby. But at the same moment, all I could feel was pain . . . pain from the area of my groin. *Very severe pain!* Stella was frantically trying to save our baby by pulling her upward from under the covers. But she couldn't succeed. I realized my baby was in danger. *But all I could feel was pain!*"

Meanwhile, little Mary slept contentedly in her crib. As for George, it took about a week for his pain to subside.

"George! George! Wake up! We've smothered Mary!"

How and When to Use Humor Abroad

Using sex as a theme for humor is probably common among many cultures, but that doesn't mean that jokes about male-female relationships in the United States will travel tastefully everywhere overseas. *Be very cautious about making light of such a sensitive and possibly emotional subject.* As examples, the Arab culture teaches men to protect and shelter women, so, as in many other cultures, jokes that demean women are usually inappropriate. And the Latin "macho" stereotype has been distorted to portray a mustache-twisting, leering male chauvinist, but to most Latin males "machismo" signifies the need to be gracious, courtly, and a defender of womanhood. Therefore, when it comes to using the "S" word to generate humor while traveling abroad, proceed at your own risk.

More Advice

Any advice on this topic should, by necessity, be divided into three categories: (1) advice for both genders, (2) special advice for men, and (3) special advice for women.

Advice for both genders: Indulging in sexual liaisons while traveling overseas is—obviously—like playing high-stakes sexual Russian roulette. With the AIDS epidemic touching every country and every culture—there are between 20 and 30 million *known* cases throughout the world—unprotected sex is like putting five bullets in the chamber and leaving only one empty instead of the conventional version where the numbers are reversed. Twenty or thirty years ago, this was not the case, and sexual encounters were more common, less risky, and therefore more of an adventure than a leap in the dark. Even so-called protected sex (considered by some to be an oxymoron) can involve lifelong consequences and regrets.

Nonetheless, *vive la différence* will probably always prevail between men and women, and so we venture to offer some advice to each gender should libidos rise in compulsive intensity while socializing in some far-off land.

Advice for men: When Westerners travel abroad, they carry with them the "unspoken belief that when you're in a foreign country, you can do things that you wouldn't normally do at home," according to international officials quoted in *Business Traveler* magazine. Men tend to rationalize that "it's expected here," or "everyone does it," or "the prostitutes need money." Also, as recounted earlier in this chapter, it is not uncommon for American businessmen to be offered the services of a prostitute by their international counterparts. Or the "opportunity" may come in other forms: a late-night knock on your hotel door, call girls at bars, or escorts at nightclubs. According to *Business Traveler* magazine, in countries as far apart as Lagos and Moscow, prostitutes steal hotel room keys, let themselves into your room, and make it difficult to eject them. Companies like Xerox and Marathon Oil Company routinely brief their employees on the dangers; in addition to AIDS, you invite robbery, extortion, kidnapping, and even murder.

Advice for women: In a book I co-authored, *Do's and Taboos Around the World for Women in Business* (Wiley, 1997), we reported that the number one concern among American businesswomen when traveling in faraway lands was their apprehension about dating, sex, and sexuality. Among the dozens of experienced women travelers interviewed for that book, all agreed that when traveling overseas, businesswomen should never mix business and sex. "Don't do it!" they all warned. One explained: "Don't wash your feet in your drinking water." Further, they warned that when traveling and working abroad, flirtations, blunt questions, and outright propositions were common and to be expected, especially in the male-dominated cultures found in the Middle East, Asia, and South America. One young, attractive American woman, a journalist from New York, told me her biggest problem when traveling in those cultures occurs whenever she sits alone in a hotel lobby. "I am frequently approached by men thinking that I am sitting there for only one purpose—soliciting for sex. In their culture, that would be the only reason a young single woman would be present in a hotel lobby. Within their culture, females are not considered business or professional people."

A contributing factor is that the image of American women as seen overseas comes largely from American movies, television, and books. In those media, American women are usually portrayed as glamorous, beautiful, and promiscuous.

What to do when confronted with unwelcome advances? They are not easy to laugh off—and they are certainly not humorous! Here are some tips provided by our panel of experienced female travelers:

1. Don't be insulted if men make passes at you. In many countries, it is considered a high compliment. However, if you want to head them off, your response should be polite but firm. How do you recognize these advances? "They are basically the same all over the world," our panel of experts replied.
2. Don't be surprised if you are asked blunt, personal questions, such as "What kind of birth control do you use?" or "Would you like to have sex with me?"
3. Do wear your wedding ring if you are married. In business circles, this may be enough to discourage advances.
4. Don't drink or dine alone or late at night with male business associates. If you must dine alone in, say, a hotel restaurant, tell the maître d' that you do not wish to be disturbed; you might also carry a book or newspaper to signal you do not welcome interruptions.
5. Don't spend long periods of time alone in public places. These include cocktail lounges, restaurant dining rooms, hotel lobbies, or buses (on tours, for example). Avoid having a local male acquaintance accompany you to your hotel room on the pretense of "hospitality."
6. Do watch body language: prolonged direct eye contact, smiles, warm greetings, touching, posture, and so on.
7. Dress conservatively.

3

Interpretations

When then President Jimmy Carter paid a visit to Poland, he was accompanied by a new interpreter who had very little time to prepare. Consequently, others in Carter's party who spoke both English and Polish overheard the interpreter explain in Polish that Carter had "abandoned" the United States (instead of "left" or "departed") because he "lusted" to visit Poland. Finally, the interpreter was heard to quote Carter as saying, "I'm here in Poland to grasp your secret parts."

In international circles, one of the most difficult but respected skills is that of an interpreter. In everyday speech, the words "interpreter" and "translator" are used almost interchangeably, but strictly speaking they have different meanings. An interpreter translates *orally* from one language to another, while a translator translates the *written* word from one language to another. Whatever the term, the responsibility is a heavy one and loaded with opportunities to fall into a messy pit of mistakes, as you will see in this chapter.

In this highly skilled specialty the most admirable job is that of a *simultaneous interpreter*. These are master linguists who customarily sit in soundproof booths, earphones pressed tightly to their ears, and listen intently to a speaker addressing an audience. Then, within seconds, they must provide the meaning of the speaker's words in another language. Imagine, if you can, listening to someone talk and then, as soon as that person utters a phrase or sentence, converting his or her words into another language. Try it. It is extremely difficult to do even if both of you speak English! Simultaneous interpreters must also cope with idioms and slang in *both* languages. So tiring is this work that two interpreters must often be hired for a full day of speakers, with one relieving the other every hour or so.

With this introduction as background, here are some anecdotes involving misinterpretations, both written and oral, and all with the same result—a cream pie in the face!

Humorously Misinterpreted Words

On a business trip to China in 1976, I was approached by representatives of the government who wanted to export Chinese-made sewing machines to the United States. They wanted my advice on the English brand name they had chosen. I asked, "What do you want to call your machine?" They replied, "We want to call it 'The Ordinary Sewing Machine.'" I laughed and asked, "Why do you want to call it 'ordinary'? In English that means common." They explained that in Communist China, where everything and everyone was equal, the word "ordinary" was a good, positive word, and, in addition, it happened to be the direct translation of the Chinese name for the machine.

I patiently explained that in the United States it would be a terrible choice. I suggested they find a name with more power and glamour, ". . . like 'Supremo' or 'Olympic' or 'Supra,'" I said. This clearly bothered them, so they adjourned to consider my advice overnight. The next morning they approached me saying, "We're confused. You said that 'ordinary' would be a bad name in the United States because it means 'common.'" I nodded in agreement. "Then why," they asked, "do you have in the United States a large and very successful company called the Standard Oil Company?"

+

On one occasion I was flying on Iberia, the Spanish airline, accompanied by a Spanish-speaking business associate. I noted that all of the in-flight publications were printed solely in Spanish. I reached into the pocket of the airline seat fronting me and took out a printed folder. It was a route map showing all the air routes flown by Iberia airlines. Printed on the cover was the phrase *mapa de rutas* ("route map"). However, the typestyle of the printed words was very ornate and I thought the "r" in *rutas* was a "p." So I turned to my companion and said, "Hernando, what is a *mapa de putas?*" Unknown to me, the word *puta* in Spanish means "whore." I had asked, "What is a whore map?" Poor Hernando winced and slumped down in his seat. Other male passengers immediately dug into the seat pocket to examine this apparently new in-flight service offered by Iberia. Later, Hernando tried to gloss over my mistake by saying, "Well, at least now you know *that* word."

+

Americans visiting Germany for the first time are usually startled and amused when they see road signs along the expressways proclaiming *Ausfahrt* and *Einfahrt,* which merely mean "exit" and "entrance." Instead of linking the words with flatulence, my elderly aunt, visiting Germany for the first time, took a different perspective. Seeing all the signs for *Ausfahrt,* she remarked, "That *Ausfahrt* must be a very large city."

+

Karel Cripe donates her time teaching English as a second language. One of her students is Estella, a Mexican woman whom Karel also hires to help clean her house. During her language

*"Our new Japanese language signs
are proving to be a big hit."*

lessons, Estella was having trouble learning that in English the word "aunt" was pronounced the same way as "ant," the insect. Karel said: "Just remember they are pronounced the same way, but they mean two different things." (In Spanish, the word for "aunt" is *tia* and the word for "uncle" is *tio*.) Several days later, Karel heard Estella call out, "Karel! Karel! Come quickly! We have some uncles in the kitchen cabinet!"

+

With the rising influx of international visitors to the United States, hotels here have become more and more aware of the need to cater to their international guests. One hotel chain in South Florida decided to start with signage—specifically signs for their Japanese guests. They instructed one of their Japanese staff members to provide the word for "concierge." He gave them the Japanese characters and they had a sign produced. In the days that followed, the hotel manager was delighted to see many of their Japanese visitors huddling around the concierge's desk. A week later, the manager learned that the Japanese staffer had actually given them the word for "pimp."

ϯ

English is not the only language to suffer from translation mix-ups. They also occur within other languages as well. In the Spanish-speaking countries of South America, certain words have entirely different meanings depending on which country you are in. For example, consider the Spanish verb *coger*. In Mexico it means to "catch" or to "take," as in the phrase "I am going to *coger* a taxi." However, travel southward to the country of Argentina, and that same word—*coger*—means something entirely different: it means to fornicate! Therefore you can understand why, when I mentioned to my friend in Buenos Aires, that I was going to *coger* a taxi, he looked at me oddly and finally said: "It can't be done."

ϯ

An alarming word for Germans is the English word "gift." The proper German word for "gift" is *Geschenk*. Not knowing this, an American once sent a package to a German friend and, hoping to avoid customs duties, wrote the word "gift" several times on the outside. Unfortunately, in German, the word *Gift* means "poison."

A similar danger lies in an Irish liqueur with the brand

name "Irish Mist." In German the word *Mist* translates to our word "manure."

✝

An American friend was visiting Australia for the first time and one evening was invited to a dinner party. He was directed to a seat next to a rather beautiful woman who, according to the host who introduced them, was an accomplished artist. Turning to the woman, the American said, "Oh? Where and when do you display your works?" The woman drew back, shocked, and for the remainder of the evening pointedly avoided him. Later, he learned that in Australia the slang term for a woman's private anatomy is her "works."

✝

I once assigned an executive in my company to manage our factory in Mexico City. He was an American but he spoke Spanish fluently, and his wife had taught Spanish in our local schools, so I thought their assimilation would go smoothly. Soon after their arrival in Mexico, the wife set out to purchase some furnishings for their new home. One of her first visits was to a furniture store to buy cushions for some chairs. The Spanish word for "cushions" is *cojines,* but she made a slip of the tongue and instead said to the salesman that she wanted to see some *cojones.* That happens to be the Spanish word for "testicles." Naturally, the salesman burst out laughing. In fact, he called his fellow salesmen from the back room to explain what the *señora* wanted. They all laughed uproariously. Flustered, the American woman said (in Spanish), "I don't know what's so funny. I not only want to buy *cojones,* I want to buy some very big, firm *cojones.*"

Laughably Misinterpreted Phrases

Florence is a Frenchwoman who, twenty years ago, came to the United States as a Rotary Club exchange student. Last summer, she returned for a nostalgic visit with her American "parents." Her English was still excellent . . . with one exception. At a dinner party in her honor, she turned to her dinner partner, an American man, and said quite clearly and audibly, "I am sorry to be between your legs, but . . ." Everyone at the table gasped. Then, to Florence's consternation, they all broke out in laughter. Retracing what had happened, they discovered there is a French phrase that in English translates literally as, "I am sorry to be in between your legs"; however, it conveys the *meaning* "I am sorry to be underfoot."

"I am sorry to be between your legs."

Dennis J. Murphy of Cincinnati is a specialist in international law who has traveled abroad extensively, including a working stint in Paris. He contributed this story involving misinterpretations:

In business dealings in any country, a sense of humor can get you through even the roughest moments of a strained negotiation. When I worked in Paris I learned this lesson my first day on the job. My boss, a senior partner of a major New York law firm, greeted me on my arrival at the firm's Paris office and explained that two presidents of major French corporations were in our conference room embroiled in an extremely tense and adversarial negotiation. My client, a major French manufacturer, wanted to license a patent from the other company. All was going reasonably well, and, in spite of my scant four months of language instruction, I understood most of what was being said. At a certain moment, my client drew me aside and said, "Ask Monsieur Dupont to lower the price [of the royalty]." Thereupon, in my most serious New York lawyer way, I said, *"Il faut baiser le prix."* Dupont drew himself back and, with extreme anger displayed on his face, said, *"Qu'est-ce que vous avez dit?"* ("What did you say?") I realized I had made a terrible blunder in French, but I had no idea what it was.

The room was silent for what seemed an eternity. I wanted to crawl under the rug. But then that wonderful French sense of humor came bubbling forth, and Mr. Dupont began laughing. He laughed and laughed and laughed, until my client, too, was laughing. All at my expense. The negotiation was rapidly concluded, with a few droll references to "that American lawyer."

Not having any idea of what I had said, I took leave of my French client. The senior partner asked me how I had handled my first negotiation in French. As I recall, I told him it was "a piece of cake."

Later that afternoon, I asked my French teacher the meaning of *baiser.* After some initial French horror at my question, she politely explained that it was a slang term meaning "to fornicate." I had confounded two closely similar French words, *baiser* and *baisser,* the latter meaning "to lower," as in "to lower the price." What I had said to this distinguished French business leader was, "Go f—— the price."

✝

An educator from Clinton, Wisconsin, once traveled to Japan to study the educational system there. Working through a translator, he explained to his Japanese hosts that he was "tickled to death" to be visiting them. His hosts looked at him oddly, conversed among themselves intensely, and then continued on with the discussion. Later, he learned that the interpreter had said in Japanese that he had "scratched himself until he died" in order to visit them.

✝

Paul is a six-year-old French boy who accompanied his mother on a trip to the United States to visit American friends. Paul spoke little English but quickly became friends with the dog belonging to his American hosts. However, Paul would become frustrated whenever he would say to the dog, in French, "Come here! Come here!" because the dog would not react. He complained to his mother, who explained that the dog only understood commands in English. Paul was amazed at this, saying, "I didn't know there were English-speaking dogs!"

✝

Sigal, an Israeli girl, was in the United States learning English when she turned to her friend Andrea and said, "One thing I don't understand about you Americans is that when you get really, really mad, you say such a *beautiful* phrase." Andrea pondered that for a moment and then said, "I don't understand. What do you mean?" "Well," Sigal explained, "when many Americans get very, very mad, I have heard them say, 'Sun on a beach!'"

*"When Americans get very angry,
why do they say such a beautiful thing?"*

The Funny Process of Interpretation

Dr. Paul Odlin is an orthopedic surgeon in my hometown who travels with his wife, Barb, to Mexico, where he donates his medical skills to local hospitals. Barb is a teacher of Spanish, so when necessary she translates for Paul. On one of their days away from the hospital, Paul and Barb visited the local out-door market. An attractive wooden carving caught Paul's eye and he asked Barb to inquire how much it cost. The merchant answered, in Spanish, that the cost was 200 pesos. Knowing that it was common to bargain over purchases in this particu-lar market, Paul instructed Barb to offer the man 100 pesos. The merchant shook his head and replied in Spanish, "one hundred and eighty pesos." Paul upped his offer, through Barb, to 120 pesos, and the bargaining and haggling continued back and forth. It became so intense that Barb found herself lagging behind in translating between the two men. Finally, she sud-denly realized the two men had *passed one another.* Paul was now offering *more* than the vendor was asking, and the vendor was asking *less* than Paul's bid. She held up both hands to the men and explained what had happened; the two men meekly agreed on a median price, and Paul walked away with the carving.

✝

A business friend of mine travels to Japan occasionally to make presentations to various business groups. For these pre-sentations, he hires a local interpreter to provide consecutive interpretation. In this system, the businessman speaks a few sentences and then waits for the interpreter to explain in Japanese what he has said. After one of these sessions, an American friend who spoke and understood Japanese said, "Do you know what the interpreter said at the beginning of your speech?" The friend then explained that after the Amer-ican started speaking, the interpreter said the following in Japanese:

"American businessman is beginning speech with thing called joke."

(Pause while the American continued.)

"I don't know why, but American businessmen always begin speeches with jokes."

(Pause while the American issued a few more sentences.)

"You won't understand the joke, so I won't tell it to you."

(Another pause for the American to continue.)
"Polite thing to do when American finishes is to laugh."
(Pause)
"I'll tell you when he finishes."
(Pause)
"He's almost done."
(Pause)
"Now!"

The Japanese audience was so polite, they not only laughed uproariously but they also gave him a standing round of applause. After the speech, the American said to the translator, "Wow! I've been giving speeches in this country for several years . . . and you are definitely the best joke-teller I've ever employed!"

✝

Much has been written about computers taking over the task of translating, which is, indeed, happening, but often with serious gaffes. For example, the phrase "out of sight, out of mind" was entered into one of these programs and it came out as "invisible thinking."

Also, at some point in the future, these computerized translations not only will be perfected but will very likely respond to the *spoken* word as well as the written word. However, even that might create problems. For example, the phrase, "Give me a new display," spoken in English might be understood by the computer as, "Give me a nudist play."

✝

In August 1990, a multilingual sign was installed outside St. Louis's Lambert Airport. The sign said "Welcome to Missouri" in seven different languages and was intended as a simple gesture of international friendship.

Unfortunately, it used incorrect spelling in three of the seven languages. It is no wonder that Paul Simon, former U.S. senator from Illinois, in lamenting America's poor skills in foreign languages, suggested that we should install signs inside all of our international airports saying: "Welcome to America. We do not speak your language."

✝

Bill Holloway was a salesman who lived and worked in the Hawaiian Islands. On one occasion, his company held a national sales meeting in Honolulu attended by the company's president. At one of the cocktail sessions, Bill found himself among a large group gathered around the top executive, who suddenly turned to Bill and said, "Bill, you've lived here in Hawaii for many years . . . I assume you can speak Hawaiian pretty well. Right?" The others in the circle knew that Bill couldn't speak a word of Hawaiian and waited to see how he would reply. Embarrassed at being singled out among his peers and not wishing to admit that he did not speak Hawaiian, Bill decided to bluff his way through and so he answered, "Yes." "Well, then," the president said, "speak some Hawaiian for me." Whereupon Bill rattled off what sounded like pure Hawaiian for thirty seconds or more. The president patted him on his back and said, "That's mighty impressive. Good for you. We need salesmen who can adapt and speak the local languages." After the president left, several of Bill's friends rushed over to him. "You don't speak Hawaiian," one said. "What did you say?" Looking a bit sheepish, Bill wiped his brow and said, "I named all the streets in my neighborhood here in Honolulu."

✝

Rikke was sixteen years old when she came from Denmark to the United States to spend four weeks with our family. She is the daughter of a very close business associate who had hosted our daughter in Denmark the previous summer. Rikke had visited the United States when she was a small child and had studied English in school, so she spoke the language well, but most of the sights and sounds were new to her. I met her at

O'Hare Airport in Chicago and as we drove on to the interstate highway, I could see she was soaking up everything around her. An Illinois state patrol car happened to move alongside us in the next lane and Rikke quickly said, "Oh, that's a state patrol car, isn't it?" When I affirmed that was correct, she continued, "And they are not allowed to cross state lines to arrest people, are they?" Once again, I said that was true, but I added, "How in the world did you know that, Rikke? Many Americans don't know that." Smiling and looking very self-satisfied, Rikke replied, "I saw it in the movie *Bonnie and Clyde*."

＋

When consultant Tom Newman was trying to impress his host in Italy by using his poor Italian, his friend commented: "Now I know how bad my English sounds!"

Pronunciation

Two Japanese tourists were on an auto tour in southern California. As they approached the San Diego region, they saw a sign indicating they were entering La Jolla, the beautiful suburb north of San Diego. One asked the other, "I wonder how Americans pronounce the name of this town?" First, they speculated that it would be "La Golla" with a hard "g." Then, they thought it might be "La Golla" with a soft "g." Finally, curiosity winning them over, they decided to stop and ask. They entered a restaurant, approached the clerk, and said, "We are sorry to disturb you. But please, very slowly, tell us how you pronounce the name of this place." The clerk answered very carefully, "Daireee Queeen."

＋

Pronunciation in American English is, indeed, a huge problem for people trying to learn our language. Hernando Cardenas claims, "English is so terribly difficult because of its delicacy and inconsistency in pronunciation." When asked to explain, Cardenas offered this quiz: "What do you Americans call the animal that gives us wool? (Answer: sheep.) What do you call the white material you sleep between? (Answer: sheets.) What do you call the small pieces of wood that fall to the ground when you carve something? (Answer: chips.) What do you call something that does not cost much? (Answer: cheap.) What is another word for boats? (Answer: ships.)" After several more examples like these, Cardenas concluded: "You see? All of those words are so similar in sound. And we know that you have one other similar-sounding word that is terribly rude—which we want to avoid—so we tend to avoid anything that comes close!"

Silly Misinterpreted Signs

A popular pastime among world travelers is collecting examples of mangled misinterpretations. In fact, such lists are now being exchanged on the Internet. Also, it seems every six months or so, some newspaper reporter or wire service discovers or rediscovers this category of worldly gaffes and publishes an article about them. With apologies for including any you may already have read, here are some of those mistranslations of signs from local languages into English that have appeared in various public media:

- From a sign posted in Germany's Black Forest: "It is strictly forbidden in our Black Forest camping site that people of different sex, for instance, men and women, live together in one tent unless they are married with each other for that purpose."
- From a Soviet weekly: "There will be a Moscow Exhibition of Arts by 15,000 painters and sculptors. These were executed over the past two years."
- On the menu of a Polish hotel: "Salad a firm's own make;

limpid red beet soup with cheesy dumplings in the form of a finger; roasted duck let loose; beef rashers beaten up in the country people's fashion."

- From a brochure from a car rental firm in Tokyo: "When passenger of foot have in sight, tootle the horn. Trumpet him melodiously at first, but if he still obstacles your passage then tootle him with vigor."

- From a German bar: "Ladies are requested not to have children at the bar."

- An American manufacturer of shoes once filmed a tribesman from Kenya for one of its commercials. The man was filmed looking into the camera and saying something in his native language about his hiking shoes. The English subtitle that appeared stated the company's ad slogan. It was later learned that the actual translation of the man's words were: "I don't want these. Give me big shoes."

- According to a professor at the University of Sonora in Hermosillo, Mexico, a 1993 Spanish version of the Arizona driver's license manual contained these statements:

  "Drivers must attend the funeral wakes of children."

  "Drivers who have donated their eyes, hearts, and other organs may ask to have their organs returned to them at any time."

  "Drivers must ensure that infants are constructed to certain specifications."

- A zoo in Budapest warns: "Please do not feed the animals. If you have any suitable food, give it to the guard on duty."

- A Swedish furrier once advertised: "Fur coats made for ladies from their own skin."

- At the United Nations, an interpretation error occurred during a speech by the ambassador from Iraq. He intended to say his nation's enemies were "liars, people of small stature," and hypocrites. The translation came out as "pygmies," which prompted an immediate protest by the ambassador from Zaire.

- Two signs were observed in a Majorcan shop entrance:

  English well speaking.
  Here speeching American, too.

- In a Tokyo hotel: "Is forbidden to steal hotel towels please. If you are not a person to do such thing is please not to read notis."
- In a Belgrade hotel elevator: "To move the cabin, push button for wishing floor. If the cabin should enter more persons, each one should press a number of wishing floor. Driving is then going alphabetically by national order."
- In a Bucharest hotel lobby: "The lift is being fixed for the next day. During that time we regret that you will be unbearable."
- In a Tokyo bar: "Special cocktails for ladies with nuts."
- In a Japanese hotel: "You are invited to take advantage of the chambermaid."
- In a Russian cemetery: "You are welcome to visit the cemetery where famous Russian and Soviet composers, artists, and writers are buried daily except Thursday."
- In a Copenhagen airline ticket office: "We take your bags and send them in all directions."
- In a Zurich hotel: "Because of the impropriety of entertaining guests of the opposite sex in the bedroom, it is suggested that the lobby be used for this purpose."
- Advertisement for donkey rides in Thailand: "How would you like to ride on your own ass?"
- In a Swiss mountain inn: "Special today—no ice cream."
- In a Bangkok temple: "It is forbidden to enter a woman even if a foreigner if dressed as a man."
- In a Belgian dry cleaner's: "Men: For best results, drop trousers here. Ladies: Leave your clothes here and spend the afternoon having a good time."
- In an English bathroom: "Toilet out of order. Please use floor below." So people did.
- In an Acapulco hotel: "All the water in this hotel has been personally passed by the manager."

- Outside a Hong Kong dress shop: "Ladies have fits upstairs."
- Detour sign in Japan: "Stop: Drive Sideways."
- On the door of a Moscow hotel room a few years back: "If this is your first visit to the USSR, you are welcome to it."

Cunning Cognates

When learning a foreign language, we receive great assistance from words called "cognates." That term refers to words in different languages that have common origins or are derived from the same root. For example, the Spanish word *vacaciones* means "vacation," and is not too dissimilar from the French word *vacances*. Sprinkled throughout other languages, and particularly Spanish and French, are familiar-sounding words that can be easily divined, memorized, and then used. For example, consider the following Spanish words: *trágico, suscripción, puntual, oscuro, invención,* and *edición*. It does not take much imagination to assume (correctly) that they mean, respectively: tragic, subscription, punctual, obscure, invention, and edition.

Having made that point, I'll now give you the bad news. There are also some words that *seem* like cognates but in fact have entirely different meanings. They are called "false cognates." In French they are called *faux amis,* meaning "false friends." For example, a woman exporter from California once told me about a time when she was selling her products in Mexico. Her knowledge of Spanish was good but not perfect. In describing one of her products—a type of jam—she wanted to say that her product used certain important preservatives. Not knowing the exact word for "preservatives," she took a reasonable guess that it would be *preservativos*. She realized she'd guessed wrong when her male customers all burst out laughing. The men then explained that *preservativos* in Mexican Spanish meant "condoms." (She later learned that the proper Spanish word for "preservatives" was *conservadores*.)

Here are some more confusing cognate stories.

☩

I once convened a meeting of Latin American managers in Cartegena, Colombia, to discuss budgets and marketing plans for the next fiscal year. We hired local buses to carry our group from the hotel to our meeting rooms and then to dinner each evening. In Colombia, such small-sized buses are called *busetas*. Unfortunately, for our colleagues from Brazil, where Portuguese is the national language, that same word refers to the female genitalia. Thus, you can imagine the consternation among the Brazilians whenever we would loudly announce, "It is time to board the *busetas*."

☩

In Spanish, the verb "to bother" (as in "I don't want to bother you, but . . .") is *molestar*. My good friend Stewart is an American who has lived much of his life in Mexico. Consequently, he was totally fluent in both Spanish and English. Stewart once confessed to me that he had neglected to learn that the English cognate "to molest" carried a much stronger meaning than "to bother." Shaking his head in regret, he said, "I bet somewhere along the line I've innocently said in some English-speaking situation 'I don't want to molest you, but. . . .'"

☩

Maria, a lovely Mexican woman, is married to an American, and they now live in Houston where she works for the Port of Houston. "My English is good," Maria told me, "but occasionally I get tripped up by Spanish words that are almost identical to English words but have different meanings." She said, "For example, I went to the doctor several weeks ago because my head and sinuses were terribly stuffed. When the doctor asked,

'What seems to be the problem?' I explained that my nose was constipated. After a few moments of compete confusion and then laughter, we both learned that in Spanish the word *constipado* is used for both conditions: congestion and constipation."

+

In German, the word *drei* is pronounced "dry" and means "three." Therefore, it's possible that you, as an American, could be in a bar in, say, Frankfurt, and order a "dry martini" and the bartender would serve you three martinis. And if you ask for a martini in Italy, it's likely you will be served vermouth, because Martini is a brand name for vermouth.

Here are some other dangerous cognates in German:

- *Sensibel* seems similar to the English word "sensible"; however, where in English it means "level-headed," in German it means "sensitive."
- The word *lust* in English almost always has a sexual connotation, but in German it is used to mean "in the mood for" as in going out to dinner, to the movies, and so on.
- The German word *sympathisch* would seem to be related to the English word "sympathetic"; but instead of meaning "a sharing of feelings," in German it simply means "likable."
- *Der Test* in German means "a quiz," but Germans also use the word *Quiz* to mean a "guessing game."
- Peter Hoyng was born in Germany but now teaches German at a university in the United States. On one occasion his car broke down, and translating literally from German, he phoned an American mechanic to advise that his car had "broken together." It took several moments of complete confusion to repair that cross-lingual mess.

+

By now you can readily understand that interpreters and translators have a highly responsible role. They must convert and convey words, but, more important, they must also convey meanings. On occasions, they must absorb a stream of words and sentences and then make a critical decision as to whether they should relay each and every word or draw a conclusion. One of these situations involved my own company, The Parker Pen Company.

The president of a well-known Japanese pen company once requested a meeting with the president of Parker Pen at our home headquarters in Wisconsin. I was serving as assistant to the president at the time, so he asked me to accompany him for the luncheon meeting. As it happened, the Japanese executive did not speak English, so he had hired an interpreter in Chicago to accompany him. As background you should know that Japan is a highly coveted market for writing instruments, but at that time the Japanese government had placed what we thought were unreasonably restrictive tariffs on the importation of all American-made pens. As we settled in for lunch and exchanged pleasantries, my boss decided it was appropriate to ask a critical question. He said, "The United States has very low duties when Japanese pens are imported into our country, but in comparison your government has placed what we consider to be unreasonably high duties on our exports to Japan. When might this be changed?" The interpreter relayed our question, and the Japanese executive began to respond. The interpreter listened and listened . . . and listened some more, making no attempt to tell us what our visitor was saying. Our salad came, and the interpreter motioned for us to begin eating. The salad plates were removed, and our main dish was delivered. Still, the Japanese executive continued his discourse in Japanese. Finally, as we were half-finished with our entrée, the Japanese man stopped his soliloquy and turned to his food. Anxiously, we turned to the interpreter, "What did he say about when the barriers will be reduced?" The interpreter merely shrugged his shoulders and said, "He doesn't know."

End of visit. We never did learn exactly why the Japanese president had requested the meeting.

How and When to Use Humor

Inaccurate translations have probably been the source of humor since the time of Alexander the Great—and before! *The objective, however, of this chapter is to demonstrate that while mistakes are both common and humorous, it is best if they don't happen to you!* If and when they do occur, there are only two solutions: (1) discover the misinterpretation and correct it, and (2) be able to laugh about it.

More Advice

Interpreters can be hired in advance in almost any major city overseas. Check with a U.S.-based foreign language agency for names, addresses, and phone/fax numbers. Or contact the U.S. Embassy or Consulate in your destination city for lists of interpreters. Be certain to explain that you'll need someone familiar with American English as opposed to British English. If you are traveling for leisure, establishing a good relationship is fairly easy since it will very likely be on a one-to-one basis. However, interpreting in business situations is more complex. Here are some tips for businesspeople who plan to work with interpreters:

1. Meet with the interpreter in advance. Get acquainted. Explain something about yourself and your business. Since you will likely be using consecutive interpretation, the interpreter will be listening during this breaking-in period to your pronunciation, accent, pace, modulation, and word emphasis.
2. Review any technical terminology you may be using. Each of us has his or her own lingo. For example, one business executive with a U.S. metals company used the word "pickling" to describe a chemical treating process. His German interpreter stopped and asked for a few moments to check his dictionary. Finding the definition,

he passed it along to the German customer who responded through the interpreter, "Why does your chemical treating process use cucumbers?"

3. Speak clearly and slowly. Try to construct your messages in groups of short, compact sentences. If the subject is complex, repeat and explain your point in several different ways.

4. Use visual aids wherever possible. Educators advise that we learn more quickly via visual than auditory signals.

5. Don't interrupt the interpreter. Interruptions can be disruptive and harmful. Also, don't be concerned if the interpreter seems to spend a longer time repeating your point than you did in presenting it.

6. Don't expect your interpreter to work for over two hours without a rest period. Interpreting is an arduous mental task that requires special concentration and therefore can be very fatiguing.

7. Be courteous and considerate. Make certain your interpreter is treated courteously, is introduced to everyone present, and is allowed time to enjoy a meal.

8. When making a speech using consecutive interpretation, consider that it will take twice as long to deliver through an interpreter. Practice with the interpreter before your speech so you can develop a rhythm and agree on mutual signals for speeding up, slowing down, or whatever.

9. If you are told that simultaneous interpretation will be used for your presentation, try to provide the interpreters (in advance) with a written text. If that is not available, meet with the interpreters ahead of time and alert them to any special technical terms you may be using, difficult concepts, or stories that rely on topical humor or a play on words. Also, try to provide them with advance copies of any slides or other visual material you will be using.

10. If confusion arises during your business discussions, ask the interpreter for advice. A good interpreter knows more than just how to translate from one language to

another. He or she may detect other problems or mis-understandings by the tone or reaction of the other person.

11. In business discussions, summarize and confirm all agreements (or disagreements) in writing. Don't rely simply on verbal conclusions as a record. Either confirm your discussions in writing before you leave or via fax or mail when you return home.

4

Protocol

In the United Kingdom, the Queen annually bestows royal honors on deserving subjects. One classification is known as the Order of the British Empire, and recipients are thereafter allowed to print those initials—OBE—following their name on all their correspondence and business cards. One American, unfamiliar with this custom, glanced at the business card handed to him by his British visitor, Mr. L. J. Richards OBE, and spent the rest of their visit together referring to the man as "Mr. Obee."

The word "protocol" comes from the Greek language and it means, literally, "the glue." It is therefore used in the context that certain agreed upon customs and rules for behavior are "the glue that holds societies together." Another less scholarly definition of protocol comes from speaker Herbert Prochnow: "Protocol is the ability to yawn without opening your mouth." Proper behavior, or protocol, has obviously been considered important through the ages because books on social etiquette first started to appear as early as the thirteenth century in Europe.

Today, proper protocol can vary from culture to culture. In the United States, Emily Post and her successors, Miss Manners

(Judith Martin) and Letitia Baldrige, have provided Americans with hundreds and hundreds of pages of instructions on what is proper and what is not. In the United Kingdom, the book of choice is called *Debrett's Etiquette and Modern Manners* (London: Headline, 1992), subtitled "Correct Behaviour for Every Sphere of Social and Business Life." And among the Chinese it is said that Confucius wrote the first book on proper behavior five centuries before the birth of Christ.

This introduction is just a brief exposition on protocol. Specific advice on proper behavior around the world will be found at the end of this chapter. Meanwhile, here are some examples of protocol gone awry, often with amusing results.

The Dutch are known for having a razor-sharp sense of humor. For this story, it is important to know that during World War II, when the Germans occupied the Netherlands, they confiscated all of the bicycles in that country. This action was a major blow to the Dutch because in a country with a complete absence of hills, bicycles were, and still are, a major source of transportation.

In 1985 I visited the manager of our company in Germany, Willi S., accompanied by our distributor for the Netherlands, Evert T. Both men were of an age to have lived through World War II. Also, Evert was known to possess a sometimes wicked sense of humor. As we were walking the German city streets, I was startled to hear—completely out of the blue—Evert stopping Willi and casually asking: "Oh, by the way, Willi, I've been meaning to ask you for a long time—have you got my bicycle?" Then, to continue the charade, Evert glanced over at a metal rack holding about a dozen bicycles and added, "Just a moment. I think I see one over here that looks like mine."

Note: Not long after this incident, at a soccer contest between teams from Germany and the Netherlands, Dutch spectators held up a huge sign asking WHERE ARE OUR BICYCLES?

Among the Japanese, the customary greeting is to bow to one another. Many Americans have difficulty with this gesture, because bowing suggests subservience. But it is important to know that in Japanese society, the act of bowing expresses humility and respect, and—as many veteran American businesspeople have come to conclude—showing humility and respect is perfectly acceptable and important anyplace in the world. However, one American who had lived in Japan for many years said he became so accustomed to bowing that even when talking on the telephone he found himself bowing to the other person at the end of the line. "It was then I knew maybe it was time for me to return to my own culture," he said.

One evening, in a busy terminal at the Los Angeles airport, I observed a touching example of this unique Asian custom of bowing as a greeting. I watched as a beautiful little three-year-old Japanese girl slowly wandered toward a group of lively and somewhat demonstrative Americans. The girl stood silently in the middle of the passageway staring at the Americans until, one by one, they began to take notice of her. Then, very slowly and silently, the tiny girl offered a perfectly timed bow. The Americans, captivated by the charming gesture offered by the little girl, turned, two and three at a time, and

bowed in return. Everyone within sight of this touching incident immediately broke into spontaneous applause.

✝

One of life's final forms of protocol involves death and dying. However, consider this rather bizarre incident as reported from Cairo in July 1997: A man who was pronounced dead regained consciousness after twelve hours in a morgue refrigerator and began shouting for help. The cold of the refrigerator apparently revived the man, Abdel-Sattar Abdel-Salam Badawi. "I opened my eyes but couldn't see anything, I moved my hands and pushed the coffin's lid to find myself among the dead," a newspaper quoted Badawi as saying. Badawi shouted for help and eventually three hospital aides who had come to remove Badawi's body found him alive. Whereupon, at that very moment, one of the employees collapsed in shock and died!

✝

Another story appeared in the newspapers several years ago about an archbishop from Italy who was making his first visit to the United States. His protocol advisers in Rome warned him about the American media. "You will probably be met at the airport by members of the media," they advised, "and reporters in America like to ask tough, even embarrassing, questions. Therefore, be extra cautious and discreet." When the archbishop disembarked at JFK Airport in New York, sure enough, he was greeted by a handful of reporters, and among the questions he was asked was: "How do you like the looks of American women?" The archbishop, realizing this was one of those dangerous questions, simply replied, "Oh? I've just arrived. Are there any women in America?" Everyone laughed, but the next day one newspaper featured a photo of the archbishop with the caption: "Archbishop's first question on arrival at airport is, 'I've just arrived. Are there any women in America?'"

✝

Ian Kerr is British born and an expert on protocol and public relations. Among his clients has been the prestigious British firm Rolls-Royce. As a result, Kerr is often asked to make presentations to diverse groups. After one of these speaking engagements, the master of ceremonies thanked him and commented that he had presented "a Rolls-Royce type of speech." Kerr told me that he was flattered until he later realized that the two main characteristics of a Rolls-Royce automobile are that they are, first, inaudible, and second, last forever.

✝

On my first visit to Nairobi, Kenya, I was greeted at the airport on a Sunday morning by The Parker Pen Company's distributor, a short, robust Englishman named Peter Davis. Even though I had been up all night on an overnight flight from London, he took me directly to the local polo field. "You shouldn't go to bed yet," Peter explained, "and, besides, I want to introduce you to Kenya and our unique lifestyle. This morning I'm playing in a polo match against some Royal Air Force chaps. They've challenged us to a contest. They've flown themselves and their ponies all the way from Cairo." We arrived at the sporting club and I observed spectators in tweed jackets or flowing dresses lining the veranda of the clubhouse, sipping pink gins and chatting as if they were at a palace lawn party back in London. On the playing field, the two teams were racing up and down the field, vying to hit the wooden polo ball. However, there was not one blade of grass on the field, with the result that all the spectators could see was a pack of horses followed by a gigantic cloud of dust racing first to the right, and then back to the left. For much of the time, the players were completely obscured. I never did see the goalposts. It was the most un-British scene I had ever witnessed.

Later, while driving me to my hotel, Davis commented: "You'll find that we English colonialists are different from the British you've been dealing with back in London." "How so?" I inquired. He explained as follows: "In most British upper-class families, it is the custom for the eldest son to inherit the family land and any titles that may go with it. So he remains in England. The second son is expected to enter either the military or the church and find his career there. The third son, who is often the 'black sheep' of the family, is usually shipped out to the colonies and subsidized by a monthly remittance of money. That serves two purposes: it gets him out of the way, and it allows him to find his own path in life. Thus, people like me are called 'remittance types,' outcasts who, as settlers, have become a different breed—tougher, more independent, and a bit coarser than your typical British aristocrat."

I asked Peter to give me an example of how this special British society behaved differently. He said, "Well, recently a friend of mine came home and found his wife in bed with another man. The other man got out of bed and beat *him* up for disturbing them!"

How and When to Use Humor

Faux pas in the area of protocol can be especially funny (e.g., falling off the dais a la Chevy Chase) but usually not at the time they occur. Spilling your bowl of soup on your female dinner partner might be considered funny days and weeks thereafter, but at the moment it happens it is a protocol disaster. It is only later that we might be able to laugh at ourselves along with the others around us. Another possibility is that we may breach protocol—and not know it!—which provides witnesses with a source of merriment after the fact and at our expense. As we have stated elsewhere in this book, there are two cardinal rules for proper etiquette, behavior, and protocol. The first is to do your homework: try to learn as much as you can, in advance, about the customs and practices of the culture you are visiting. The second rule is never, ever do or say anything that will bring unfavorable attention or embarrassment to another person. In other words, *humor at another person's expense is never appropriate wherever you may travel.*

More Advice

Whether you travel on business or as a tourist, proper decorum is valued all over the world, and especially in Asian countries. In Japan, for example, style (i.e., the *way* things are done) is just as important as substance. The act of giving a gift is a perfect example of this trait. The Japanese are very generous with gift-giving, but the way a gift is presented, the way it is wrapped, and its nature are also very important. For example, in Japan a gift should be presented with both hands; paper wrapping should be used, but not white paper (because it represents death and rebirth); and four of anything is considered bad luck (because the word "four" is *shi* in Japanese, which also means "death").

Social behavior is also important in Japan. When seated, a balanced pose with both feet on the ground is favored; and when standing or making a speech, putting one's hand in one's pocket is considered too informal. An aberration to all this formality occurs during long, late-night drinking parties favored by Japanese businessmen. This is when decorum may be thrown to the wind and it is permitted to overimbibe to the point of drunkenness. It is also when frank or even unkind comments might be made. But the remarkable thing about this contradiction in behavior is that the next morning everything that was said and done the night before is forgiven.

Another important aspect of protocol and decorum throughout the Asian countries is the matter of "saving face." Very simply, this means you must never do or say anything that might bring embarrassment to another person. Carrying it one step further, any act that brings *humiliation* upon another person would be the worst form of insult and injury.

Turning to other countries and cultures, we can see that proper etiquette is also highly valued and respected in places like France and England. The word "etiquette" comes to us from the French language, and England's Lord Chesterfield is regarded as the father of modern-day etiquette. Proper behavior is so prized in England that in my four years of daily commuting there, where people were thrust together in hot and stuffy train carriages each day, suffering through delays and bad weather, I heard only *one* verbal disagreement between two passengers. And that resulted because one of the passengers claimed that after some minor breach of behavior, the other person had not apologized properly.

As for proper speech—volume, content, word selection—in international circles, a world-wise businessman once gave me this valuable piece of advice: "At all times speak as though your wealthy, elderly aunt had just asked you how much you think she should leave you in her will."

In summary, when traveling overseas whether as a tourist or on business, as a student or in the military, the wise traveler will "mind his or her three Ps"—patience, perseverance, and politeness.

Here are more samples of some of the differences in manners around the world.

Punctuality   As a rule, we Americans tend to be fairly punctual. However, in countries like Germany, Austria, Switzerland, and Sweden, punctuality is more precise and extremely important. To be even a few minutes late is a breach of etiquette. The opposite is true in Latin America and much of Southeast Asia—time is considered a long, flexible flow, characterized by an attitude of "Why live our lives in measured segments?"

Table manners   When at a dinner table, most Americans follow the rule of eating with the right hand holding the fork or spoon while resting the left hand in their lap. In countries like Germany, Austria, and Switzerland, it is considered improper to rest the left hand in one's lap. Both hands should remain above the table, resting the wrists lightly on the table edge. And throughout the Middle East and Southeast Asia, it is improper to eat using the *left* hand. That is because the left hand is used for bodily hygiene (i.e., there is often an absence of toilet tissue in public bathrooms).

Eye contact Americans, and many other cultures, prefer direct eye contact, especially when greeting one another and during conversation. However, in countries like Japan, Korea, and parts of Southeast Asia, it is considered rude to look directly at another person for more than a few seconds. Interestingly, the Native American culture taught the same thing: it was considered rude to look elders squarely in the eyes.

Greetings Americans and Western Europeans are taught to shake hands, usually with a firm grip and direct eye contact. In Japan, the customary greeting is to bow at the waist. We Americans are often uncomfortable with that action, since we tend to regard bowing as an act of subservience. However, in Japan, bowing signifies humility and respect, not necessarily subservience. In places like India and Thailand, people greet one another in a different manner—by pressing the palms together as if praying, and dipping the head slightly. They are saying, in effect, "I pray to the God in you." In parts of Africa, they greet one another by spitting at the other person's feet. Maori tribesmen in New Zealand rub noses, and in Tibet people stick out their tongues as a gesture of greeting.

Touching The Japanese are not "touchers." They would be surprised and upset if you—as a business traveler or as a tourist visitor—hugged or clapped your arm around their shoulders, just as you might do to a friend on a sports playing field. An irony, however, is that one impression many Americans have when visiting Japan for the first time is how crowded everything seems: streets teem with people, stores are filled with customers, and when people ride trains or subways they are packed in shoulder-to-shoulder, almost nose-to-nose. Anthropologist Edward T. Hall explains that the Japanese countenance these periods of extreme closeness and touching by mentally removing themselves. In other words, they can mentally separate themselves from the actual situation.

At the opposite end of the touching spectrum are the South Americans, followed by Middle Eastern men, then Italians, some French, and the Russians. All of these nationalities seem to enjoy bodily contact of some kind, whether it be man-to-man or woman-to-woman. Among good friends, greetings usually involve a body hug accompanied by a few hand pats to the upper back. In social conversation, South American men will stand very close together—only inches apart. One man may gently grasp the other man's elbow, or even finger the lapel of his suit. In the Middle East and parts of Southeast Asia, two men may walk along a street casually holding hands. This is nothing more than an act of friendship and respect. South American, Italian, Russian, and French men will also greet their male friends with a warm hug, called in Spanish-speaking countries the *abrazo*. We North Americans fall in the middle of these two extremes.

$$\pm$$

These are just a few samples of varying protocol around the world. Happily, today there is more and more information available on this subject. One excellent source for information on greetings, gestures, dining, clothing, and lifestyle—country by country—is called *Culturgrams*. It is a collection of 164 four-page leaflets, one for each country, published by the Kennedy Center Publications, Brigham Young University, P.O. Box 24538, Provo, UT 84602-4538. Cost, at this writing, is $80.00 for one unbound set and $100.00 for a bound set. Phone 1-800-528-6279 for more information and for a current catalog of publications.

5

Exporting American Humor

An old Chinese proverb says: You get sick by what you put in your mouth, but you can be hurt by what comes out of your mouth.

Every culture enjoys some form of humor. As I said in the introduction, "Laughter has no accent." But humor has difficulty crossing cultural boundaries because what is humorous in one country is often not humorous in another. The French philosopher Blaise Pascal, gave voice to this truism when he said three hundred years ago, "What are truths on one side of the Pyrenees are untruths on the other side."

Different Types of Humor

Steve Allen, comedian, author, and musician, writes: "Every culture, every town, every individual has his or her own sense of humor." Allen spoke with comedians in **China** and found that the same types of jokes—stories about relationships between husbands and wives, young people and old people, and city and rural dwellers—were considered funny in both the Chinese and American cultures. Yet in other cultures, where these relationships are taken perhaps more seriously, the same stories fail to evoke even a smile. Allen cites an example where a Jewish audience was told a joke about frugality and the person who was the butt of the joke was named Ginsburg. The result was silence. But before another Jewish audience the same joke was told where the person was named MacTavish, and everyone laughed.

Are there cultures that are humorless? Columnist Russell Baker claims that the **Germans** have absolutely no sense of humor—which he said during a TV interview with a trace of exaggeration in his voice, exaggeration being a favorite form of humor. The truth is that Germans in the south of the country (Bavarians) are known for their generally more outgoing personalities, love of music, and celebrations such as Oktoberfest. Northern Germans, in contrast, are considered more serious and stoic. Perhaps Baker has spent most of his time in the north.

Among the **Japanese,** anything—anything whatsoever, even the slightest word or action—that brings attention or embarrassment to another person is considered not only unfunny but a social taboo. This breach of manners leads to the condition called "losing face."

While some cultures seem to have smaller and different funny bones than others, hardly anyone would like to be characterized as "having no sense of humor" (except, perhaps, for the TV character Mr. Spock of *Star Trek,* who never laughs). Also, humor can take different forms. There is satire and there is bitter satire. There are sexual jokes and there are degrading sexual jokes. Allen points out that comedy can also be about tragedy. The underlying subject matter of many jokes, sketches, comedy films, and plays is quite serious. For example, the **British** have staked out a hilarious form of stage humor in their frenetic bedroom farces, but the subject matter usually deals with the subject of infidelity—a serious matter in any culture.

Silent humor can be more effective crossing cultures than spoken humor. Cartoons, pantomime, and slapstick can, of course, cross over easily. Visit your local library or bookstore and you'll very likely find books of captionless cartoons from artists all over the world. As for pantomime, the late stage and motion picture comedian Danny Kaye captivated audiences on several continents without knowing a single word of the local language; all he used was his physical humor. And with slapstick, the films of the Three Stooges throwing cream pies by the dozens can evoke laughter regardless of the nationality of the audience.

American humor, in oral or written form, is difficult to carry overseas for two reasons: it is often either *topical,* or it relies on a *play on words.* Our parlor stories, locker-room humor, and Jay Leno's most recent monologue are all difficult to repeat successfully when traveling overseas or hosting international visitors because each relies on the listener's intimate knowledge of American English and American current events. One test to determine one's ability to truly comprehend American humor is to read cartoons in the *New Yorker* magazine. Another is to understand and enjoy the humor of cartoonist Gary Larson, of "The Far Side" fame.

Where Humor Can Be Difficult—Even Dangerous

When it comes to spoken or written humor, you'll find that in many international circumstances—especially in business or politics—it can occasionally be counterproductive, even harmful. For example, the *Foreign Service Journal,* a magazine published for foreign affairs professionals, reports, "Humor in the Foreign Service is as hard to find as a plumber on Sunday." The magazine also says: "Next to treason, making an inappropriate joke may rank as the second most taboo practice in diplomacy."

In spite of this concern, members of the diplomatic profession are divided on the role of humor in statesmanship. On one side, many diplomats dislike reinforcing the stereotype of the straight-backed, humorless government servant; on the other side, many are aware of incidents where attempts at humor were misunderstood and backfired. The latter cadre of public servants avoids humor because when it comes to foreign relations, stakes can be high. Even former president John F. Kennedy is reported to have said, "You can always survive a mistake in domestic affairs, but you can get killed by one made in foreign policy."

American humor is extremely difficult to export because we so often rely on current events and wordplay. We are not alone in that respect. Each culture has inside jokes that outsiders cannot understand. Hume Horan, a retired foreign service officer, explains that **Arabs,** for example, like to make put-downs about people in the next village or neighboring apartment. **Egyptians** prefer political humor. **Danes** tend to use heavy sarcasm. The **British** are often stereotyped as stiff and humorless, yet over the years, some of the most successful television comedy shows in the United States have come to us from England. The plot and characters for *All in the Family,* surely a classic of American comedy, were drawn from a popular English TV show of the 1960s called *'Til Death Do Us Part.* Broad comedy, such as slapstick, is also popular in England and has been exported frequently to America—just consider Benny Hill, Monty Python, *Fawlty Towers, Are You Being Served?* and other such comedy programs that have been successful on both sides of the Atlantic.

Having said all this, I do think that on occasion it may be possible (but still dangerous) to relate your favorite joke by tailoring it to local tastes. For example, in a country that views the French as possessing a reputation for arrogance and puffed-up pride, this story may be permissible: It seems some years ago when Mikhail Gorbachev, George Bush and François Mitterrand were the leaders of their respective nations, they found themselves aboard an airplane accompanied by a hippie and a priest. When the pilot announced that they had suffered engine failure, the five men discovered there were only four parachutes. Gorbachev announced he had to save himself because he was the most powerful leader in the world, so he grabbed the first parachute and jumped out. Bush, moving just as quickly and claiming the same privilege, took the second parachute and jumped. Mitterrand clutched the third chute and said, "Everyone knows I'm the smartest leader in the world, so I should naturally claim the third parachute," and he, too, jumped. The priest turned to the hippie and said, "I'm an old man. Save yourself and pray for our souls." Whereupon the hippie replied, "No sweat, pop. We still have two chutes left. The smartest man in the world just jumped out with my sleeping bag on his back."

Certainly in the foreign service, jokes like that are akin to playing catch with a hand grenade. Yet without humor, duty in some remote post must be trying. *Foreign Service Journal* reports that when one disgruntled American ambassador attended an official dinner and was seated below a foreign dignitary whom he outranked, he sent a message to his home office complaining about "a frightening crisis." His superior directed that a three-word response be sent in reply: "Laugh it off." Ironically, the official in the department codes office reported there was no secret symbol for "laugh."

Even U.S. presidents have, figuratively speaking, slipped on banana peels. Remember reports of Ronald Reagan's 1994 radio broadcast when, thinking he was just testing his microphone, he casually announced that he had "signed legislation that will outlaw Russia forever. We begin bombing in five minutes." Humorous, yes . . . but also dangerous stuff.

One encouraging and amusing incident occurred in 1996 involving Madeleine Albright, at that time ambassador to the United Nations. When the Cubans shot down an unarmed U.S. civilian plane off the coast of Miami, she severely criticized Fidel Castro by saying, "Frankly, this is not *cojones* (balls), this is cowardice." President Clinton later commented that hers was the most effective one-liner in foreign policy during his administration. Albright was later named secretary of state in the Clinton administration.

A Few Funny Stories That Travel Well

In four clever lines, Ogden Nash succinctly expresses our natural curiosity over what makes other cultures tick.

A Crusader's wife stole from the garrison
To have an affair with a neighboring Saracen.
She was not oversexed, Nor jealous or vexed.
She just wanted to make a comparison.

✝

Public speakers in America are expected to begin their talks with one or two amusing stories. At this writing, former U.S. Secretary of State Lawrence Eagleburger is relating this story when he speaks before groups of Americans: It seems that God called Bill Clinton, Boris Yeltsin, and Benjamin Netanyahu to heaven and proclaimed, "I have called you here because I have some bad news. Because of runaway sin and corruption, I am going to destroy earth. As leaders of your countries, I want you to go back and warn your people."

Clinton returned to earth and immediately went on national TV, saying: "I have some good news and some bad news. First, the good news. There *is* a God. He exists. I have met Him and talked with Him. The bad news is that because of our sins He is going to destroy our world."

Yeltsin also appeared on national TV in Russia, saying, "I have some bad news and some *worse* news. First, the bad news. Even though most of us are atheists, I have met and talked with God. So, there is a God. The worse news is that because of our sins He is going to end life on Earth."

Netanyahu appeared on Israeli TV and announced to his people, "I have some good news and some *better* news. First, there is a God. I have met and talked with Him. The better news is that there will never be an independent Palestinian state."

✝

Although American humor can be complex, here are two stories that seem to translate well and have successfully crossed cultural and language barriers. A Lebanese friend and business associate told me this first story: To start, it is important to know that the Lebanese consider themselves among the most experienced world traders. This is because of their Phoenician heritage. As students of history know, the Phoenicians were the first of the world's great tradespeople. Even before the time of Christ, they were the first to venture out into the Mediterranean to conduct commerce with other nations around the shores of that great sea.

The story goes that a worldwide commission was appointed to recruit the first humans to fly a spaceship to Mars. The commission began, naturally, by interviewing an American astronaut. Among the first questions asked was, "How much would you charge to fly to Mars?" The American pondered for a few moments and then replied, "I would require ten million dollars because it is so risky and I would want my family protected in case of an accident." The commission members then turned to a Russian cosmonaut. "How much would you charge?" He responded, "Twenty million dollars." "Why twenty million dollars?" was the obvious rejoinder. The cosmonaut explained, "Ten million for me and ten million for the state, because that is the way we do things here in Russia."

Next, the commission sought a Lebanese because of his ancestors' long history as brave explorers. "How much would you charge?" they asked. The Lebanese stroked his chin, considered the matter carefully, and then declared, "*Thirty* million dollars." "Why thirty million?" he was asked. "Oh, it's very simple—ten million for *me,* ten million for *you* . . . and ten million for the American to make the trip!"

✝

The second story deals with the true meaning of the French phrase *savoir faire*. Literally, that means, "to know how to do something." But among the French, it signifies much more than that: diplomacy, grace, coolness, aplomb, and other such admirable qualities. In fact, many of the French believe they have a special, secret gift for *savoir faire* that other nationalities do not possess.

Frustrated by the French appropriation of *savoir faire*, and while attending a meeting of global executives in Phoenix, Arizona, I found myself in the company of three French businessmen and decided to seek an explanation. "I know the

French believe they have a special claim to *savoir faire* that other cultures do not understand or appreciate," I said, "but tell me what *savoir faire* really means—what is the true meaning of that phrase to a French person?"

They all responded with typical Gallic shrugs. But one, who also was the youngest, said: "That is *très difficile,* but I will try to explain it by using an illustration. Let's say a man comes home from work and finds his wife in the arms of another man. If he quietly turns around, closes the door, and leaves . . . *that* is French *savoir faire.*"

The second Frenchman, somewhat more mature, shook his head and objected. "No, no, no. You are almost correct, but you have not captured the *true* meaning. To use your example, if that man comes home and finds his wife in the arms of another man and then says, 'Oh, excuse me. Please continue.' And then, if he turns around, closes the door, and leaves . . . that is true *savoir faire.*"

The third Frenchman was the oldest and appeared to be the wisest. He merely shook his head and said: "No. That's still not it. And to explain, I will use your example. The man comes home, finds his wife in the arms of another man, says, 'Excuse me. Please continue.' He turns and walks away. Now, if that other man *can* continue . . . that is true French *savoir faire.*"

✝

Another reason American humor is difficult to export is because the English language is so difficult. Our grammar is complicated; we use idioms, slang, jargon, buzzwords, and acronyms; and we love to invent new words and catchphrases. But what makes our language especially difficult for others to learn are the inconsistencies in pronunciation and spelling. Incidentally, the opposite is true of Spanish. Spelling and pronunciation are easy in Spanish because the sound of each letter of the Spanish alphabet is constant. Spelling contests are a rarity in Spanish schools; once you learn the sound for each letter, you can spell any word that you can hear and vice versa— when you see a word, you can pronounce it.

"Excuse me. Please continue."

To dramatize how English is inconsistent in both spelling and pronunciation, and also to use as an amusing game, take the poem appropriately titled "English Is Tough Stuff." It was sent to me by an engineer in Portugal who had read my book *Do's and Taboos of Using English Around the World* (Wiley, 1995), where I stressed that English was extremely difficult for others to learn. He agreed with that premise and as further evidence sent me this poem. Here's the challenge: Read the following aloud . . . without stumbling once. After you've tried, give it to friends and see how they perform.

English Is Tough Stuff

Dearest creature in creation,
Study English pronunciation;
I will teach you in my verse:
Sounds like corpse, corps, hearse and worse.
I will keep you, Suzy, busy,
Make your head with heat grow dizzy.
Tear in eye, your dress you'll tear;
So shall I! Oh, fare well, fair.
Just compare heart, beard, and heard,
Dies and diet, Lord and word,
Sword and award, retain and Britain,
(Mind the latter, how it's written).
Now I surely will not plague you
With such words as vague and ague,
But be careful how you speak:
Say break and steak, but bleak and streak,
Cloven, oven; how and low;
Script, receipt; shoe, poem, toe.
Hear me say (naught here is trickery)
Daughter, laughter, and Terpsichore;
Typhoid, stoic; topsails, aisles;
Exiles, similes, and reviles;
Scholar, vicar, and cigar;
Solar, mica; war and far;
One, anemone; Balmoral,
Kitchen, lichen; trauma, laurel;
Gertrude, German, wind and mind;
Scene, Melpomene, seen, and signed;
Billet scarcely discards ballet;
Bouquet, wallet; mallet, chalet;
Blood and food are not like stood,
Nor is mould like ghoul and would;
Viscous, viscount; load and broad;
Toward, too forward to reward,

Bard leads his leaden tongue among
His Muse's mews, is lead unstrung.
Pain reigns unreined—just ask your psyche:
Is a paling stout and spiky?
Won't it make you lose your wits,
Writing "groats" and saying "grits"?
It's a dark abyss or tunnel,
Fraught with rot like rowlock, gunwale;
Islington, but Isle of Wight,
Housewife, verdict and indict.
Tell me: which rhymes with "enough":
Though, through, plough, cough, thorough, tough?
Hiccough has the sound of "cup,"
Enough of this stuff—give it up.

How and When to Use Humor

In this chapter, we have learned more about the vagaries and fickleness of American humor when carried abroad. As you read, some in the U.S. diplomatic corps would admonish, "Don't even think about it!" While that seems excessive, I hope the basic message throughout this book is emerging cleary—namely, that it is difficult to export our American humor. That does not mean we should be humorless. It suggests, however, that while traveling overseas we should exercise caution if tempted to retell the au courant joke back at the office, or offer what we think will be a witty and clever rejoinder or remark. Whether as a business traveler, a vacation traveler, a student abroad, or anything else, *the intelligent voyager will try to slowly divine what makes people laugh in the culture being visited.* Here are some suggestions on how to accomplish that: Gently ask acquaintances what type of TV comedy they favor. Read local magazines and newspapers and observe how humor is treated in them. Engage in conversation with closer friends: "What is your impression of American humor? Is it too bold, too raucous, too complex? How would you describe *your* brand of humor?" Ironically, while you are discovering new facets of that particular culture, you are also building better relationships through that miracle potion called "understanding one another better."

More Advice

In my own travel experiences over a period of thirty-five years, I have learned that people everywhere like to laugh, but it is difficult and even unwise to transport your favorite jokes abroad. It goes without saying that you wouldn't tell a Polish joke in Poland. Yet, ironically, many nationalities have their own special ethnic targets at which to hurl barbs. Belgians, for example, like to tell stories about the ignorance of their neighbors, the Dutch. And the Dutch return the favor with similar stories about the slow-wittedness of the Belgians. The Irish and the English do the same. And while working and traveling in Italy, I was told that you can take any so-called Polish joke and simply convert it for an Italian audience by saying, "There was this fellow from Cuneo . . . ," which happens to be a small village located outside of Milan. When I asked, "Why Cuneo?" my friends shrugged and replied weakly, "We don't know. We just like to make jokes about people from Cuneo." Even in the tiny country of Lebanon, I heard my associates tell jokes about "this fellow from Homsy . . . ," which I later learned was a small town in the mountains, south and east of the capital of Beirut. Once again, why Homsy had such an unfortunate reputation was not clear.

Another lesson I learned about humor between cultures was taught to me by George Parker, former president of The Parker Pen Company. "The written word does not smile," he cautioned. What he meant was that when writing letters or business reports, what we think is clever or witty composition is often not interpreted that way when read by someone for whom English is a second language.

It is also important to know that some cultures smile—or laugh—at seemingly inappropriate times. In places like Thailand and Malaysia, people may smile or even giggle to cover anger or when hearing sad news. My friend Richard Gesteland observed this phenomenon during a tour of duty in Singapore. When he learned about the death of his mother, his housemaid, a Malay, smiled. A week later, news came that his father had also died. The maid actually giggled, but he realized it was her way of covering up a terribly uncomfortable situation. The Japanese will smile to mask embarrassment. The Japanese are also taught to remain unsmiling when official photos are taken, such as when applying for a passport or a driver's license. They do so because in their culture smiling shows a lack of respect for authority. This rule even applies when children pose for photos with Santa Claus. Also, displaying the wide open mouth is considered crude in Japan, which explains why people in both Japan and China are taught to cover their mouths with a cupped hand when laughing.

When it comes to using humor overseas, the best advice is to "tread on tiptoes." Here are a few suggestions:

- Avoid retelling the most recent "canned" jokes heard over the bridge table or in the locker room. They were undoubtedly conceived for American ears and American funny bones.
- Avoid any and all ethnic jokes. Your international associates will assume that if you'll tell one unflattering story about another ethnic group, you'll also tell one about them.
- Watch to see what types of subjects, situations, or incidents amuse your hosts or your international visitors. Then, if you want to try to inject humor, carefully emulate those.
- If and when you commit some goof or gaffe, be certain to laugh it off. This demonstrates that you can laugh at yourself, which is usually an admired quality in almost any culture.
- Humorous devices such as English malapropisms, puns, or spoonerisms definitely do not travel well. A malapropism is a humorous misuse of word; a pun is a play on words; and a spoonerism (named after the Reverend William Archibald Spooner) is when we transpose syllables (e.g., instead of saying "Ronald Reagan popularized jelly beans," we say "Ronald Reagan popularized belly jeans").
- Finally, avoid all smutty jokes, scatological comments, and so-called four-letter words.

6

Gestures

The Dini Petty Show is one of the most popular daytime talk shows on Canadian national television. Ms. Petty was once interviewing me on her show and said, "The gesture in your book that I liked most was this one" (and she tapped her two forefingers stiffly on a tabletop). When I confessed I didn't recognize that gesture, Petty said, "Oh, it's in your book! You said that in Egypt it means 'I want to go to bed with you.'" I corrected her, saying, "No, no. You go like this," and I held my forefingers outward and tapped them against each other. Petty quickly rejoined, "Well, no wonder I didn't have any fun there!!"

When we travel overseas, we communicate in many ways—with our words, our behavior, our body language. In fact, anthropologist Edward T. Hall claims that fully 60 percent of our daily communication is unspoken. However, the problem is that many gestures and some of our body language can be easily misunderstood. The reason is that not all gestures send the same signals; it depends on where you are. For example, the single, best-known gesture in the United States is the sign for "OK" (thumb and forefinger forming a circle, with the other three fingers pointing upward). In France, however, this can mean "zero" or "worthless." Several years ago, I took a hotel room in the south of France and the concierge asked me if my room was satisfactory. I replied by making the "OK" sign. Disappointed, he responded, "Oh, sorry. If you don't like the room, I'll find another." Then in Japan, this same sign is used to signal "money"—the circle is interpreted as the shape of a coin. And in Brazil, don't use it! It is considered a terribly rude gesture, since it represents a part of the female anatomy. When Richard Nixon was vice president in the 1950s, he visited Brazil, and as he deplaned in Sao Paulo he unknowingly flashed not one but two (!) "OK" signs. His gaffe was photographed and appeared in newspapers across Brazil.

A comprehensive listing of gestures and body language from around the world appears in my book *Gestures: The Do's and Taboos of Body Language Around the World*, which appeared in 1998 in a new, revised and expanded edition. Lengthy excerpts from this book have appeared in the *New York Times* (1996) and *Reader's Digest* (1997). Also, cultures other than our own are apparently interested in this subject because the first edition of this book has been—or will be—printed in eleven other languages. Following are some more anecdotes from that book.

✝

In 1993, former late-night TV host Arsenio Hall referred to the *Gestures* book in his opening monologue. Hall chastised the author for listing the "three most popular gestures in America" as: (1) the "OK" sign, (2) the "V" for Victory sign, and (3) the thumbs-up signal. Hall said, "I think Roger is missing a very important one—you know, the one we see out here in Los Angeles on the expressways. It's kind of signaling 'We're Number One' . . . but with a different finger."

✝

On a separate occasion, when Johnny Carson hosted his own popular late-night talk show, he read excerpts from *Gestures*, including this one: "It says here that in Japan, don't stand with your hands in your pockets . . . or, for that matter, in anyone else's pockets!"

✝

In an interview describing life at the White House, former First Lady Barbara Bush described being seated at a state dinner next to Russian president Boris Yeltsin. Later she learned that during the dinner Yeltsin had turned to his interpreter and asked, "What does it mean in the United States when a woman places her foot on a man's foot?" adding that "In my country it means the woman loves the man." The reason for Yeltsin's query was that, without realizing it, Mrs. Bush had been grinding his foot into the ground with her own foot. Later, Yeltsin autographed his menu with this note to Mrs. Bush: "You stepped on my foot, you knew what it meant, and I felt the same way."

✝

There are definitely specific and strong rules for using gestures and body language. We observe them rigidly, sometimes without even being aware of them. The best example of this in the United States, and in certain other countries, involves behavior while riding on an elevator. It has been proven by scientists using hidden cameras that when only one or two people ride on an elevator, they usually lean against the walls of the elevator. If four people are aboard, they usually move toward the four corners. However, when the population reaches five or six people, everyone begins to obey more complex rules of elevator etiquette. It is almost like a ritualistic dance. They all turn to face the door. "They get taller and thinner," as psychologist Layne Longfellow describes it. "Hands and purses and briefcases hang down in front of the body—that's called the Fig Leaf Position, by the way. They mustn't touch each other in any way unless the elevator is crowded, and then only at the shoulder or lightly against the upper arm. Also, there is a tendency to look upward at the illuminated floor indicator. If they speak, it is definitely *sotto voce*."

Proper behavior on an elevator is sacred.

If you doubt this is standard—almost sacred—elevator behavior, then try this test (if you have courage): Next time you enter a crowded elevator, *don't turn around and face the door.* Instead, just stand there facing the others. If you want to create even more tension, put a silly grin on your face. Very likely the other passengers will glare back, surprised, grim, and upset. The reason? You've broken the rules. I did this on one occasion and I heard a man at the back of the elevator whisper, "Someone call 911. We've got a real weirdo here."

When I related all this to my son, at the time a psychology major at the University of Texas, he expressed disbelief. "Is that really true? I'll ask my professor about it." A week later, he called back excitedly: "Dad, it works. I told my professor and we decided to make it a class experiment by trying it on office buildings here. We've got people freaking out on elevators all over town! And we've got one guy who has *added* something." "Added what?" I asked. "Well, he does like you said, stands staring at them, gets them all upset and nervous, and then just before the elevator doors close . . . he jumps *backward* off the elevator! Then he runs up to the next floor. And when the doors open, he tells them, 'I heard what you said about me!'"

More Silly Stories about Gestures

This actual event occurred in the Vatican, in Rome: Moments after being blessed by Pope John Paul II, Jan Lavric, a visiting doctor from London, stunned bystanders by abruptly standing up, getting out of his wheelchair, and walking away. Observers thought they had witnessed a miracle.

Lavric explained later: "Before our audience with the Pope, we were waiting in an outside reception room. I was tired, so I sat down in an empty wheelchair. Suddenly, a nun wheeled me off, and before I could explain, the Pope blessed me."

✝

Gestures can also be a valuable form of opinion polling. According to *People* magazine, at least one U.S. politician has his own system of gauging his popularity. "I watch the crowds waving to me," he explained, "and I count the number of fingers they're using."

✝

Throughout Latin America and in parts of Europe, good friends often greet each other by hugging. In Latin America, the hug as a greeting is called an *abrazo,* or "embrace." My first encounter with this custom occurred in the airport at Buenos Aires, Argentina, when I was very new to the game of greetings and gestures. There to meet me, arms outstretched, was the manager of our local company. "My God!" I thought, "that man is going to hug me!" My life seemed to pass before my eyes. Walking forward stiffly, I forgot that one must move the head either right or left. We ended up smashing noses.

✝

In Japan, businesspeople invariably greet one another by exchanging business cards. But in Japan, the business card is treated with great respect—even with ceremony. The Japanese will offer their card by holding it carefully with the thumbs and forefingers of *both* hands, accompanied by a slight bowing of the head. The printing on the card will be positioned toward the recipient, who will receive the card (again, with *both* hands) and carefully—very carefully—read the information. The recipient will then place the card on the table in front of him or her for future reference. The reason for this solemnity is that the card represents that person's *identity,* or persona. Americans are much more casual about exchanging business cards: a quick reception with one hand, a hasty glance at the card, and then it often goes into a pocket. Some Americans may slip it into their wallet and pants back pocket, which could greatly offend the Japanese! After all, you will then *sit* on that pocket containing the other person's *identity* card. Americans may also unthinkingly take out the Japanese person's card and *write* on it!—a second transgression. But the worst incident I have witnessed is when one bored American businessperson casually reached into his shirt pocket, removed the Japanese person's card, and absentmindedly *picked his teeth* with it!

✝

Let's say you want to *beckon* someone. Here in America, we would very likely hold out our hand, palm upward, and repeatedly draw the hand toward our chest. Or we would hold our hand up, palm facing our body, and curl one forefinger up and down. The latter is an insult in places like Malaysia because there it is used only for beckoning animals. And throughout Europe the customary way to beckon someone is to hold out the hand and arm—palm facing downward—and then make a scratching motion with the fingers. To beckon a waiter in, say, France, the normal motion would be to make eye contact and then bob the head backward ever so slightly. In Colombia, several soft handclaps will bring the waiter to your table. Probably the most unusual way to beckon a waiter, however, is found in Mexico. There patrons use a *kissing* sound— that's right, they make a rather loud kissing noise with the mouth and lips. Common sense says that in other countries you should exercise extreme caution in using that signal! It should definitely be avoided at truck stops across the United States.

✝

There is one gesture that has at least a half-dozen completely different meanings depending upon where you are in the world. The gesture is this: Hold your arm up and away from the body, with the hand about head high. Make a fist, and then extend the index and little fingers stiffly upward. Your hand and two fingers are creating a U shape. In baseball, an umpire will do this to signal "two outs"; in football, the referee uses it to signify "second down." Throughout the state of Texas, this signal is called "hook 'em horns" and refers to the mascot and symbol of the University of Texas, the longhorn steer, and your hand signal represents the horns of that animal. In Italy, it is a very rude gesture—called the *cornuto* (for horns of the bull)— and sends the message that your spouse (especially your wife) is being unfaithful. You are being cuckolded! In parts of Africa, this gesture places a curse, and in places like Los Angeles, street gangs may use this sign—representing Satan's horns—as a recognition symbol. Finally, in Milwaukee, Wisconsin, home of numerous foundries and metal-fabricating factories, coarse barroom humor gives it still a different meaning. "In our taverns," Milwaukeeans explain, "when you see someone hold his hand up like that with only the two outward fingers standing upright, it simply means that a veteran, long-suffering punch press operator is ordering four beers."

✝

"Bartender! Four beers!"

When my grandson, Timmy, was five years old, like other children his age, he would respond to the question "How old are you?" by holding up his hand and extending his five fingers. When asked to count the fingers, he would quickly say his numbers: "One, two, three, four, five." One day, a friend asked him: "Now. Can you count backward?" Timmy thought about this for a few seconds, then turned around so his back was facing the questioner, extended his hand, and proudly recited: "One, two, three, four, five."

Another story about children and their numbers involves a family of Americans who travel extensively due to the father's occupation in international business. Accordingly, they stay in scores of different hotels and the children have come to regard a hotel as a second home. However, the parents were mystified whenever their youngest child, a girl, would recite her numbers. She would successfully reach the number ten and then say "eleven, twelve, fourteen, fifteen . . ." and so on. It finally dawned on the mother that the youngster was learning her numbers *while riding on elevators,* where it is the custom to omit the thirteenth floor because it is considered bad luck.

One Dozen "Be Careful" Unintentionally Funny Gestures

Whether you are traveling for business or pleasure, here is a list of one dozen "be careful" gestures in certain countries.

1. Be careful in **Germany.** The "OK" sign is a rude signal because it refers to a body part. Chewing gum in public is also considered impolite. And if you are driving on the autobahn and another driver points his forefinger to his temple and rotates it, he is sending you a strong message that you are a lousy driver . . . in fact, it is so strong *he can be arrested for making that gesture!*
2. Be careful in **Japan.** The "OK" signal there is also used to signal the word "money" or, more specifically, "change." It means you want your money in the form of change.

Also, watch your posture—correct posture is both practiced and expected. That means don't sit with your feet propped casually on a coffee table, or slouch in an easy chair, or stand with your hands in your pockets.

3. Be careful in **Italy**. We've already described the *cornuto*—index and little finger extended upward—which means your spouse is unfaithful. Placing the thumbnail under your two front teeth and flicking outward is a strong insult in Italy. In fact, in Shakespeare's play *Romeo and Juliet*, it resulted in a duel between the two opposing families and, indirectly, led to the deaths of the two lovers.

4. Be careful in **Thailand**. Never pat anyone on the top of his or her head. The Thai people believe that is where their spirits reside.

5. Be careful throughout the **Middle East** and **Southeast Asia**. Never expose or point the sole of your shoe at another person. That is a grievous insult, because the sole of your shoe is the lowest and dirtiest part of your body.

6. Be careful in **Argentina**. When pouring wine, never serve it with your left hand, or rotate your wrist backward, thus pouring the wine backward over your hand with the thumb pointing up.

7. Be careful in **Russia**. When entering a theater or auditorium and walking through the row to take your seat, always face the people already seated. If you face the stage, you are being impolite by passing your derriere directly in front of their bodies or faces.

8. Be careful in **France**. A unique gesture there is to form a circle with the thumb and forefinger, place it over the nose and make a twisting motion. Among the French, that is the signal that someone nearby is drunk.

9. Be careful in Europe. In homes there, bathroom doors are customarily kept closed, whereas in America we tend to keep them open to signal that they are free for use. Therefore, in Europe you should knock on the bathroom door to determine if it is being used. And speaking of knocking, in **Mexico** avoid rapping on a door or table

top with the often-used "dum-de-de-dum-dum . . . dum-dum" (or rapping to the old musical phrase "Shave and a haircut . . . two bits"). In Mexico, this particular series of beats carries a very crude and rude message.

10. Be careful in **Chile.** If you happen to make a fist with one hand and slap it upward into the palm of the other hand (as we might do while standing idly on a street corner), you are sending the signal "Up yours!"

11. **All over the world,** watch for spatial differences. This warning refers to the varying degrees of space different cultures prefer when standing next to one another. According to anthropologists, we all have invisible "bubbles of air" surrounding us. That is our space, our territory. We become uncomfortable when someone invades our space by standing too close to us. For example, in Western Europe and the United States, our "bubbles" are about eighteen inches thick; when combined with the bubble of another person, that becomes thirty-six inches or, significantly, *an arm's length away.* In the Far East, people prefer even larger distances. But in the Middle East and Latin America, the bubbles are smaller. Two men from those regions will very likely stand very close to one another, at least by Western standards. As a result, visitors to Latin America claim they can often observe what they call "the conversational tango." This occurs when an American, unfamiliar with this custom involving closeness, is confronted with a Latin who, quite naturally, stands very close. Uncomfortable, the American is inclined to step backward. The Latin, not understanding why the American is moving away, naturally steps forward. The American takes another step backward. The Latin moves forward. And this shuffle continues on and on. Observers claim they have seen this type of duo "dance" across an entire room, hence its name, "the conversational tango." Watch for it.

12. **In most countries,** the "forearm jerk" is known as an insulting and inflammatory signal. It is done by bending the arm at the elbow, making a fist with the hand, and

smacking the edge of the other hand down into the crook of the elbow. It symbolizes the phallus and is saying, in effect, "Up yours!"

How and When to Use Humor

Once again, as in previous chapters, the humor evoked from gestures and body language invariably comes from *mistakes*—using a gesture or series of signals that in the country you are visiting, signify the exact opposite of what you intended. Once that yin-yang has been discovered, it can result in laughter all around. But left unexplained, it can also tarnish or even ruin a relationship. *Once again, the desired pattern here is to proceed cautiously.* Don't, for instance, attempt to be amusing in Japan by proclaiming, "I understand you Japanese don't like it when we look you squarely in the eyes, so I'll look at the floor while I'm here! Hah, hah, hah." Nor should you try to outdo a South American, Italian, or Russian with an overexuberant embrace. And speaking of greetings, one business traveler I knew decided he would outshine the local Frenchmen with their gallant hand-kissing. At a large social gathering, as he progressed down a receiving line, he noted that each Frenchman greeted the hostess by gently kissing the back of her hand. Showing that Americans could do one better, he grasped the woman's hand, turned it over, and planted a wet kiss on her palm! Surely that was the first time in French history this act of greeting had ever been done in that fashion.

More Advice

Advice for this category of cross-cultural communication is simple. "Use the two A's." That means to apply two words that begin with "A." They are to be "aware" and, when in doubt, "ask."

Being aware begins with doing some homework. Fortunately, there are more and more reference books available on the subject of international body language. The bible is, perhaps, a book called *Manwatching*, written by the famous English anthropologist Desmond Morris. This book was first published in 1977 by Harry N. Abrams, Inc., New York. A more recent book by Morris is titled *Bodytalk: The Meaning of Human Gestures* (Crown Trade Paperbacks, 1994).

Then, as you travel abroad, be more aware of the human signals going on all around you. If something strikes you as unusual or unconventional, ask a local person about the meaning of that signal. Some of my friends have made the mistake of visiting a new country and boldly asking, "What unusual gestures do you have here?" Of course, the response is: "We don't have any strange gestures. *You* have a few I don't understand, but we don't have any." A better way to open a friendly investigation of this subject is to start, perhaps, over dinner. Introduce the subject by saying, "I read recently about different gestures around the world. For example, in America, if we wanted to beckon the waiter, we would do this (raise the hand slightly and waggle it). What do you do here?" Another conversational gambit is to talk about how Americans hold their eating utensils—cutting with the knife in the right hand, fork in the left, then laying the knife down, switching the fork over to the right hand, and forking the food into our mouths. With the so-called Continental style of eating, the fork remains constantly in the left hand and the knife in the right.

Once the subject of gestures is broached, ask your local friends what the following hand gestures mean in their country: the "OK" sign, the "V" for Victory sign, the thumbs-up sign, the way we wave hello and good-bye, the way we would beckon someone to "come over here," and so on. You'll be surprised to learn that some of these common American signals carry entirely different meanings elsewhere, and some of those meanings are both strong and rude.

7

Cruising

I once asked a veteran "cruiser" which country she enjoyed visiting the most. "Oh," she replied, "that's easy. I love visiting Italy." When I asked why, she answered this way: "Oh, I just love to visit the ancient Roman fornifications."

Cruising has become more popular than ever. The North American–based cruise industry will carry almost 5 million passengers this year. New ocean liners that resemble huge floating hotels are being launched each year. For many Americans, a cruise for one or two weeks, or even for a few days, not only provides unaccustomed luxury but also introduces them to different cultures around the world.

The initial gaffe most first-timers commit is to refer to the cruise liner as a "boat." It is properly called a "ship." The term "boat" is used for much smaller craft, such as a lifeboat or rowboat. The way to remember this distinction is to memorize the phrase "ships carry boats . . . not the other way around."

Some Humorous Cruising Stories

Cruising can generate a wide array of interesting and humorous experiences. For example, elderly passengers seem to favor the smaller luxury liners because the pace is less frenetic and the meals and programs are more suited to their tastes. Here's one description I've heard of this more mature crowd: "This is the type of group that when they order a martini, they ask to have a prune put in it."

On one of these cruises, the ship's professional comedian, noting all the wrinkles and gray hair in his audience, declared, "The average age of these passengers is deceased."

✝

Menus aboard cruise ships are known for both their abundance and their exotic foods. On one cruise in the South Asian Sea, passengers were treated to bird's nest soup, a delicacy of the region. One matronly diner stopped the chef and asked for an explanation: "Exactly how do you make bird's nest soup?" The chef described how actual birds' nests were purchased at local markets and used as the major ingredient. He also described how the birds would patiently form the nests using liquid from their beaks as a sealer. The woman asked, "You mean you are serving us something made from the saliva of birds? I won't eat that!" she protested. When the chef asked her what she would like as a substitute, she swiftly said, "Just fix me an egg omelet," not considering which part of the bird produces eggs.

✝

Many first-time cruisers are fascinated—and often confused— by the multitude of day-to-day operations of a cruise liner. Following is a list of actual questions collected and presented to me by the cruise director of the luxury liner the Royal Viking Queen:

1. "What time is the midnight buffet?"
2. "Do these stairs go up or down?"
3. "Is there an elevator that goes to the front of the ship from the back?"

4. "Do the crew sleep on board the ship?"

5. "How do you get fresh milk on the ship?"

6. One passenger called the purser's desk at 2:00 A.M. and said: "Why is the ship so dark? Does the captain know that all the lights are out in the front of the ship?"

7. "What does the kitchen do with the ice sculptures when they are done with them?"

8. "What time does the crew come on board in the morning?"

9. A passenger asked a member of the crew, "What happens when the electrical equipment breaks down and all the lights go out?" The crewman responded, "Not to worry. We have an extralong extension cord from Fort Lauderdale."

10. When greeting people for a Catholic Mass, a priest had a passenger walk up to the him and ask, "Are you the priest or the rabbi?"

"How do you get fresh milk on the ship?"

11. A passenger called the purser's desk and said frantically, "I can't get out of my cabin!" The purser replied, "Madam, have you tried the door at the front of your cabin?" "Indeed I have," she replied, "but one door goes into the bathroom and the other one has a sign hanging on the doorknob that says, DO NOT DISTURB."

12. A passenger asked a waiter, "How does the crew get on board the ship each day?" Thinking that she was kidding him, he replied, "Oh, we bring the crew over each morning from shore by helicopter." Two days later the captain received the following complaint from that passenger: "Those noisy helicopters wake me up too early each morning."

+

Here is a parlor quiz sometimes conducted aboard cruise ships:

1. Name the three most popular languages in the United States.
2. Name the three most popular languages in Canada.
3. What is the most popular man's name?
4. What is the most popular family name?

(The answers appear at the end of this chapter.)

+

One of the fringe benefits of being an author and speaker is to be booked as "an enrichment lecturer" aboard cruise ships. My wife and I have had the pleasure of doing nine of these cruise engagements in the past twelve years. One memorable trip occurred in 1993 on the inaugural cruise of the unique, twin-hulled *Radisson Diamond*. Our itinerary called for us to cruise for one week among the Virgin Islands in the Caribbean. There were 360 passengers aboard, almost all from the travel company that owned the ship, so for them it was a combination orientation and free holiday. The ship's official in charge of scheduling all entertainment activities is the "cruise director" and he informed me that I was scheduled to speak on the Monday of the cruise. Unfortunately we encountered rain for the first two days, Saturday and Sunday. This was especially disappointing because the passengers—all young people from Minnesota—were anxious to soak up some sun after a long, cold winter. On Monday, we were once again greeted by rain. My program was scheduled for 3:00 P.M. However, precisely at 2:30, the clouds broke, the sun came out, and the sea calmed. You can guess what happened. When I entered the ballroom to start my program, exactly three people greeted me: the cruise director, my wife, and the professional entertainer/comedian, who happened to be allergic to strong sunlight. The cruise director shrugged it off, saying, "These things happen. Don't let it bother you." And so for an hour we four sat around chatting. During the remainder of our cruise we were fully occupied visiting local ports, so I never did present my program.

In honor of that comedian, and with my thanks, here is one of the more memorable stories he told one evening at the cabaret show: It seems three businessmen were in a meeting—an American, a German, and a Japanese—when a slight buzzing was heard. "Excuse me," said the German, who reached into his suit pocket and extracted a pen. Removing the cap and pressing a small button, he proceeded to carry on a complete, two-way telephone conversation. The pen was, obviously, some type of new telephone transmitter. When he finished, he replaced the pen, saying, "I am sorry for the interruption." Then, pointing to the pen, he proudly explained, "This is the newest in German technology."

The three men continued conversing until a soft beeping sound was heard. This time the Japanese gentleman bowed his head in apology, reached inside his mouth, and removed a tooth. He pressed a small button on the tooth and, like the German, proceeded to carry on a conversation using the tooth as a portable telephone. After he finished, he apologized most graciously and explained, "This is the newest in Japanese miniaturization."

Time went by and the trio continued their discussion.

Suddenly, with an audible and clearly recognizable sound, the American broke wind. "Pardon me," he apologized, and then added, "I believe I have a fax coming in."

+

Cruising is not all smooth sailing. My wife and I once traveled aboard Cunard's famous *QE2* ocean liner from Southampton, England, to New York. It was in November when—unfortunately—the North Atlantic Ocean is known to experience strong storms and heavy seas. On the second day, the seas began to rock and roll. I was scheduled to deliver a program in the ship's theater and, much to my surprise, about a hundred people attended. Because the ship was rocking rather vigorously, I chose to sit in a chair and deliver my remarks. The seas worsened, and so I hurried my presentation even though the audience remained loyal and unruffled. Just before I finished, my lectern tipped over from the motion of the ship and someone shouted, "Look out!" Thinking they were referring to the lectern, I laughed . . . but then glanced to my left to see that the grand piano had broken loose from its moorings and was slowly rolling across the stage directly for me. Fortunately, I was able to jump off the stage just as the stagehands rushed to grab the piano and secure it. Everyone applauded, but I had a funny feeling they were *not* applauding my program.

This story continues. The storm worsened. We experienced 40-foot waves and 60-mile-an-hour winds. Two gaming tables in the casinos tipped over, glass and tableware could be heard crashing to the deck, and eventually the captain ordered everyone to return to their cabins. The storm continued for two solid days. We learned later that some twenty-six people had been injured.

As we finally approached the North American continent, the storm abated and the captain addressed the crew and passengers over the public address system. "I am proud," he said, "of how our ship carried us through these rather rough seas. She is a fine ship and we all should take great pride in sailing with her." My wife merely commented: "Well, I'm mighty glad he's proud of his ship. But I wish he wouldn't inject that trace of doubt in his voice when he talks about her."

Incidentally, on a later voyage, the QE2 struck a reef off the coast of New England and spent several months undergoing millions of dollars of repairs.

+

Shipboard friendships are common and often long-lasting. After two weeks of socializing, it is tempting and common to say to your newfound friends, "If you are ever visiting my part of the States, I hope you will call on us for a visit." This is precisely what happened with my friends John and Frieda on a cruise when they became friends with Martha, a widowed matron from England. The following spring, John and Frieda received a letter from Martha saying that, indeed, she was coming to America and would be traveling near their home in Wisconsin. Naturally, John and Frieda repeated their invitation to spend time with them as their houseguest.

Martha arrived the first week in May. John and Frieda hosted her royally, holding parties in her honor and taking her to a variety of local events and entertainment. Seeing that she was enjoying her visit, the couple expanded their hospitality to include nearby and even faraway tourist sites. By this time, however, it was the end of May, and Martha showed no signs of leaving. John and Frieda were becoming weary of providing this constant stream of entertainment, so one day they ventured the question, "Well, Martha, is there anything *else* you would like to see in this part of America?" Martha considered that question for a moment or two and then declared, "Yes. Yes there is. I think I would like to see the Fourth of July."

+

One particular friendship that usually develops on board a ship is between you and your tablemates in the dining room. This affiliation occurs because at the beginning of a typical cruise the maître d' assigns you to a specific table in the dining room, and you are expected to sit at that table for each meal. You can state your preferences by specifying if you wish to sit at a table for four, six, or even eight persons. After a week or more of dining with the same people, you'll find that friendships often blossom. On one of these occasions, a gentleman tablemate of mine, on learning I was the so-called enrichment lecturer on board, assured me he would attend one of my programs. When the time came, I looked around and noted that sure enough, there he was sitting in the very first row. After the program, and as we were seated around the dinner table, he remarked, "That was a very interesting program you provided—very informative and entertaining. I also enjoyed your delivery and timing, but one thing that caught my attention was that I didn't realize you *spit* so much when you spoke."

✝

The "Tourist's Prayer," which follows, was composed by Pulitzer Prize winner, humorist, and syndicated newspaper columnist Art Buchwald especially for American cruisers. It was recited at the beginning of each voyage by the cruise director of the Royal Viking *Sun* and is reprinted here with the kind permission of Mr. Buchwald.

> Heavenly Father, look down on us your humble, obedient tourist servants who are doomed to travel this earth taking photographs, mailing postcards, buying souvenirs, and walking around in drip-dry underwear.

> We beseech you, oh Lord, to see that our plane is not hijacked, our luggage is not lost, and our overweight baggage goes unnoticed.

> Protect us from surly and unscrupulous taxi drivers, avaricious porters, and unlicensed English-speaking guides.

> Give us this day divine guidance in the selection of our hotels, that we may find our reservations honored, our rooms made up, and hot water running from the faucets (if at all possible).

The Tourist's Prayer

We pray that the telephones work and that the operators speak our tongue, and that there is no mail waiting from our children which would force us to cancel the rest of our trip.

Lead us, dear Lord, to good, inexpensive restaurants where the food is superb, the waiters friendly, and the wine included in the price of the meal.

Give us the wisdom to tip correctly in currencies we do not understand. Forgive us for undertipping out of ignorance and overtipping out of fear.

Make the natives love us for what we are, and not for what we can contribute to their worldly goods.

Grant us the strength to visit the museums listed as *musts* in the guidebooks.

And if per chance we skip an historic monument to take a nap after lunch, have mercy on us for our flesh is weak.

Husbands:

Dear God, keep our wives from shopping sprees and protect them from bargains they don't need or can't afford. Lead them not into temptation for they know not what they do.

Wives:

Almighty God, keep our husbands from looking at foreign women and comparing them to us. Save them from making fools of themselves in cafes and nightclubs. Above all, please do not forgive them their trespasses for they know exactly what they do.

All together:

And when our voyage is over, and we return to our loved ones, grant us the favor of finding someone who will look at our home videos and listen to our stories, so that our lives as tourists will not have been in vain.

This we ask You, in the name of Conrad Hilton, American Express, and the Royal Viking Cruise Line.

Amen.

✝

Finally, returning from Mexico after a cruise in the Caribbean, my wife and I were placed in seats in different rows on the homebound airplane. She found herself seated next to a very distinguished looking woman, fashionably dressed and immaculately coiffed. The two women struck up a conversation, comparing their experiences while in Mexico. My wife inquired, "Did you encounter any tummy troubles?" Quizzically, the woman turned to my wife and stated, "Tummy troubles? Tummy troubles? No, I didn't have any tummy troubles. However, I did have the *shits* for three straight days."

How and When to Use Humor

This setting, cruising, is perhaps the easiest to deal with when it comes to how and when to use humor. *Just let 'er rip!* Cruises are fun! Cruises are uninhibited! People want to enjoy themselves! If certain dour passengers prefer privacy, they can hide themselves in the ship's library or on a deck recliner with a magazine covering their faces. But most of your other fellow passengers are paying big money to be able to laugh. That is why almost every cruise liner employs a professional comedian as part of its Las Vegas–style entertainment offering. In fact, comedy is so important that the comedians who regularly sail the seas usually have four or five different routines—or shows—and then they disembark to be replaced by another of their unique fraternity . . . just to keep the comedy fresh and rolling along. Add to this the fabled ship's "costume party," where you'll likely be pressured into wearing some combination of clothes you'll never don again in your lifetime, and you can understand why "How and When to Use Humor" here adds up to "let 'er rip!"

More Advice

As we said at the outset, more Americans are cruising than ever before. One reason is that they now have a multitude of choices:

- They can cruise for as little as one day or up to three months and anywhere in between.

- They can select ships that vary in length from under 200 feet to over 1,000 feet.
- They can travel with just a handful of fellow passengers or as many as 3,000.
- Finally, they can choose from a galaxy of destinations—cruises literally go wherever there is enough water to float a vessel.

Once aboard, first-time cruisers are usually dazzled by the huge array of foods, services, and activities. Stage shows rival those in Las Vegas. Menus offer unbelievable selections, and it seems food is available constantly, twenty-four hours a day. Activities include lectures, movies, bingo, exercise classes, arts and crafts classes, card games, swimming, dance lessons, deck shuffleboard, golf putting greens, and, of course, shore excursions.

If you are unacquainted with cruising, here is some basic advice:

1. Your local travel agent will have a variety of cruise catalogs, but you might also try to locate an agency that specializes in cruises. Check your Yellow Pages. Fares vary widely, so shop around.
2. When booking a cruise you'll find the fares usually include air transportation to your port of departure and from your final destination, but be sure to verify this when making your inquiries.
3. Once you are booked, your cruise line will usually advise you in advance about travel concerns such as limitations on luggage (if any), requirements for passports and visas, health and medical attention available aboard ship, accommodations for handicapped passengers, tipping practices, communication services available (most ships offer efficient ship-to-shore telephone service), smoking restrictions, laundry services, dress codes, shopping and gambling aboard ship, and so on.
4. Once you're aboard, the important people in your life will be as follows:

- The *purser* is an all-around information source for any questions you may have. He or she is also responsible for your stateroom assignment.
- The *cruise director* is responsible for all entertainment provided aboard ship.
- If you are to have assigned seating in dining rooms, the *maître d'* is extremely important. You may have a choice of being seated alone or with several other dining companions. When it comes to table companions, finding compatible people can be a toss of the dice . . . so if you are unhappy, the maître d' may come to your rescue.
- Your *room steward* or *stewardess* cares for your daily needs—cleaning, room service, laundry, and so on. Be prepared to leave substantial tips for your room attendants and your table waiters; the cruise liner usually provides printed guidelines for tipping.
- If you are an unaccompanied woman, most cruise ships have *male escorts* or *hosts* on board. These are usually retired, single gentlemen who enjoy socializing and travel and who receive free accommodations in return for serving as social hosts during the cruise. They are aboard, however, under severe restrictions: they must not show any favoritism toward any one or several women, they must never indulge in affairs or shipboard romances, and—above all— they must be very adept at dancing.

In short, cruising is usually found to be the most glamorous and comfortable way to see the world; you can relax and dine your way across the miles. In fact, a survey of 2,000 passengers by the Royal Caribbean Cruise Lines found that 95 percent of respondents rated cruises as "extremely or very romantic" compared to land-based vacations. Some 48 percent of the respondents said they had sex as many as six times a week on a cruise vacation, compared with their usual once or twice weekly at home.

Now here are the answers to the four questions posed on page 108:

1. The three most popular languages in the United States are English, Spanish, and American Sign Language.
2. The three most popular languages in Canada are English, French, and Chinese.
3. The most popular man's name (in the world) is Mohammed.
4. The most popular family name (in the world) is Lee (or Lei).

8

Business Bloopers

The Chevrolet division of General Motors named one of its models the Nova, only to learn that in Spanish the words *no va* mean "it doesn't go" . . . hardly a good name for an automobile.

My own company, The Parker Pen Company, several decades ago marketed a bottled ink called SuperQuink. It was advertised as "the ink that was proper for every social situation" because it was bright, intense, and never "feathered." The ad copy concluded: "So, to avoid embarrassment in your social correspondence, be sure to use Parker SuperQuink." The campaign was successful in the United States, so it was exported to the nearby Mexican market. Twenty thousand metal signs were imprinted in Spanish with the slogan ". . . to avoid embarrassment, use Parker SuperQuink." The direct translation into Spanish of the words "to avoid embarrassment" is *para evitar embarazo*, which is what was printed on the signs. Unfortunately, what Parker did not know is that in Mexico those words form a special idiom that translates: ". . . to avoid *pregnancy*, use Parker SuperQuink."

Visit your local college or university, enroll in a course like "Introduction to International Marketing," and you'll soon learn about scores of classic blunders committed by American companies who try to sell their product overseas.

The anecdotes related at the beginning of this chapter are told and retold year after year. Stories like these have a tendency to proliferate and become, perhaps, apocryphal. Many are true; others are perhaps questionable. Still, as the news media search for more and more entertaining stories, and as the Internet issues more and more grist, these types of stories are perpetuated. Here is a collection culled over the years from various public sources:

- An international company developed a new watchband made of solid stainless steel that could be quickly attached or removed from the wrist by one easy squeeze with the other hand. This combination of stainless steel and easy removal seemed to make it attractive to the sportsperson because perspiration would not stain the band, as it does with leather, and the easy removal feature seemed appropriate for active people. Members of the company's marketing division were instructed to "Dream up a brand name that will be attractive for a designer watchband and also convey that it is appropriate for the international sportsman." Within a week, one of the more creative employees proposed that the new product should be called "Jacques Strap." Unfortunately, his suggestion was rejected.

- A brand of beer in Australia is known as "Four X," but the makers were hesitant to introduce it into the U.S. market when they learned there was a line of condoms called Fourex already established here.

- One of my Dutch business colleagues once asked me, "I know what Preparation H is, but what ever happened to Preparations A through G?"

- The American slogan for Salem cigarettes was "Salem—Feeling Free." It got translated into Japanese as "When smoking Salem, you feel so refreshed that your mind seems to be free and empty."

- In Belgium, General Motors used a tag line "Body by Fisher," but when that was translated into Flemish it said, "Corpse by Fisher."
- Ford had similar problems in Brazil when it introduced its Pinto model. The company found that *pinto* was Portuguese for "tiny male genitals."
- An American maker of T-shirts in Miami printed shirts for the Spanish market promoting the Pope's visit. Instead of the desired "I saw the Pope," the shirts proclaimed in Spanish, "I saw the Potato."
- Hunt-Wesson introduced its Big John products in French Canada as *"Gros Jos"* before finding out that that phrase, in slang, means "big breasts."
- In Italy, a campaign for Schweppes Tonic Water translated the name into "Schweppes Toilet Water."
- Another standard that has been communicated around the international business community for many years involved Pepsi's "Come Alive" advertising slogan. It came out of the translation process in Taiwan as "Pepsi brings your ancestors back from the grave."
- Jockey underwear is widely known in the United States, but that brand name is also known and recognized in scores of markets overseas. The company that made the Jockey name famous is located in Kenosha, Wisconsin. As a result, in the 1920s the original name of the company's most popular underwear style was the Kenosha Klosed Krotch, and popular usage referred to the company as the Kenosha Krotch Company. As the company began to extend overseas, however, it did not take officials long to determine that for a masculine product—whether in the United States or overseas—the image of a jockey was far better than a "krotch."
- Chrysler's $200,000 production sports car was called the Diablo, but its original name was Countach, which, when pronounced in Italian, means . . . well, what a rude man might utter upon spying a good-looking woman.

- According to writer Harris Collingwood, when Coca-Cola first attempted to translate its name into written Chinese, the syllables sounded like either "bite the wax tadpole" or "female horse stuffed with wax," depending on the dialect.
- When Braniff Airlines translated a slogan about its luxurious upholstery ("Fly in leather") into Spanish it came out as, "Fly naked."
- In many parts of Japan, it is common for householders to raise chickens in small hutches or coops adjacent to their small, closely built homes. An American manufacturer of household deodorants reasoned that this provided a wonderful sales opportunity for its product. In searching for a new brand name, the company was tempted to call its product "Chicken Shot" . . . but cooler heads prevailed.
- Puffs tissues are known and recognized throughout the United States, but when the makers tried to introduce their product in the German market, they learned that *Puff* in German is a colloquial term for a house of ill repute.
- Frank Perdue is known in the United States as a highly successful provider of tasty chicken products. His slogan "It takes a tough man to make a tender chicken" was widely promoted and remembered. But when translated into Spanish, the literal message became, "It takes a sexually stimulated man to make a chicken affectionate."
- In Germany, where Vicks wished to introduce its line of cough drops, the company was informed that the German pronunciation of "v" is "f." Consequently, Vicks became "Ficks." Unfortunately, that word in German is the guttural equivalent of "sexual penetration."
- The famous maker of baby foods, Gerber, introduced its line in African markets using the same packaging graphics as in the United States, where the Gerber labels feature the picture of a lovable baby. They soon learned that in Africa, companies routinely put pictures on the label of *what is actually inside* the container.
- Advertising in the U.S. pharmaceutical field is customarily high-class and subtle because much of it is aimed at doctors, pharmacists, or other well-educated users. Using

one of these slick, high-quality campaigns, one firm successfully introduced a new product that provided a quick and efficient cure for intestinal worms. Based on that success, they decided also to introduce the product into certain African markets where they knew that malady was common. They ran the same ad campaign, but sales were almost nonexistent. Consulting a local African advertising firm, they were told that their U.S. advertising was too subtle; the local population did not understand their message. So the company asked that agency to provide an alternate campaign. Soon, in newspapers and magazines throughout that market, ads began appearing showing a pile of human fecal matter crawling with worms. The copy read, in effect, "If you have these, you need our product." Sales skyrocketed.

• A large toothpaste maker planned to introduce a product called "Cue" into France. As it happened, there was already a notorious pornographic magazine in France with that name.

• In China, Kentucky Fried Chicken's famous slogan "finger-lickin' good" came out as "eat your fingers off."

✝

Finally, in Japan, consumer goods products like to adopt—or adapt—English names for their products. Here are some that obviously had good intentions but didn't quite hit the mark:

• Rolls of toilet paper called "My Fannie"
• Little chocolate candies called "Choco Baby"
• A nondairy creamer called "Creap"
• A sports drink called "Pocari Sweat"

More Funny Business Blunders

Veteran international marketing executives in Europe sometimes scoff at the term "the Common Market." One of them,

Peter Ward from England, claims, "The Danes will never be like the Italians, and the Germans have very little in common with the Spanish. Therefore, it is more appropriate to refer to the European Economic Community as the *Un*Common Market." Supporting this view is cross-cultural trainer Robert Waisfisz, who as reported in the *Wall Street Journal* (June 1993) endeavors to rank nations in Europe according to their degree of individualism, respect for authority, and aversion to uncertainty. To help his business students learn about those differences, he urges them to remember, "In Germany, everything is forbidden unless it's allowed. In Britain, everything is allowed unless it's forbidden. And in France, everything is allowed even if it's forbidden."

+

The late Kenneth Parker was the son of the founder of The Parker Pen Company, and he personally designed many of Parker's products. One of his notable achievements occurred in 1939 when he designed and introduced the famous Parker "51" pen, heralded in the 1950s as one of the five best-designed consumer products in the world. It was the first fountain pen to combine plastic and metal, but more important, it featured a sleek, streamlined front unlike any pen on the market at that time. During World War II, the Parker "51" became a prized possession around the world. One reason was that hundreds of thousands of American GIs treasured their "51" pens because a writing instrument symbolized a link with home via letter-writing. Stories filtered back to Parker about American combat pilots preparing to bail out of their aircraft and reaching back into the cockpit to save their Parker "51" pen. So valued were the pens that one foreign country awarded Parker "51" pens to its military heroes in lieu of medals.

It is no wonder, then, that after the war the "51" pen was in huge demand. In fact, a bustling counterfeit market developed. During this period, Kenneth Parker visited Italy and toured retail stores in Rome accompanied by his Italian distributor. Near the famed Colosseum they were approached by a man wearing a bulky overcoat who asked: "Want to buy a Parker '51' pen? Right off the boat," whereupon the man opened his coat to reveal dozens of pens clipped into special pockets sewn into the lining. When his question was translated, Mr. Parker said to his associate: "Ask him how much he wants for a pen." When the street vendor replied, "Five U.S. dollars," Mr. Parker was certain they were fakes because the retail price back in the United States was ten dollars. After examining the pens and confirming that they were, indeed, counterfeits, he took out his business card and told his distributor to give it to the man. The distributor did so, and after examining the card carefully, the vendor looked up, pointed to Parker, and in Italian asked, "Is this *really* Kenneth Parker . . . the president of Parker Pen??" When the distributor assured him that was correct, the vendor thought for a moment and then said, "Ask Mr. Parker when he's going to introduce a *new* pen—I'm getting tired of selling this junk!"

*"When are you going to bring out a new model, Mr. Parker?
I'm getting tired of selling this junk!"*

Postscript: After this incident, Mr. Parker realized the vendor had *kept* his business card. He then envisioned the man continuing to hawk the fake pens, claiming, "Here! See this! I buy them directly from the president of Parker Pen!"

How and When to Use Humor

Mixing humor and business can be almost as problematic as in the diplomatic corps, where we learned that apparently they don't even have a code for the word "laughter." (See Chapter 5.) Nonetheless, after my thirty-five years in international business I can report that one of the most enjoyable challenges was to build *relationships* with my international counterparts, not just impersonal business contacts. And one way to do that was to laugh together! I agree with my peers who advise that doing business internationally means becoming something of a chameleon. You should always strive to adapt to your surroundings. That doesn't mean you forfeit your Americanisms or your national pride. It means you respect local customs and behaviors just as you might expect your counterparts to respect your own ethos. In other words, in cultures where grace and what we might consider "overpoliteness" prevail, adopt some of those qualities yourself. In countries with more forthright exuberance, display a bit of that, too. In countries that seem devoid of mixing humor and business, follow that lead. In summary, *international business is uniquely challenging because each culture is a challenge in itself.*

More Advice

If you are involved in a business that is thinking of expanding into international markets, here are some steps to consider:

1. Phone the nearest office of the U.S. Department of Commerce and make an appointment to visit with representatives of the International Trade Association (ITA), a subdivision of the Department of Commerce. Staff peo-

ple in the ITA have one purpose only, which is to help American companies expand overseas. They will review with you an extensive menu of services—many of them free, others available at a very reasonable cost. The ITA will help identify the most likely markets for your product and the best ways to establish contacts there.

2. As you've seen in this chapter, one important aspect of doing business overseas is establishing and protecting your brand name. Therefore, one of the first subjects you should investigate with the ITA representatives is how to gain trademark and patent protection in overseas markets for your products.

3. You will probably want to consider making one or several exploratory trips to your targeted markets to learn something about the competition there, the local pricing for your product or service, the laws governing your product or service, and what marketing methods are most common. One of the fastest ways to obtain this type of information is to attend an overseas trade show or exhibition that specializes in your product category.

4. In addition to the federal government's services via the Department of Commerce and the ITA, check with your state government. Most states also offer assistance in generating export sales, everything from low-cost financing to overseas offices staffed by people who are paid to help businesses from your state gain a foothold overseas.

5. When the time comes to produce printed materials in another language, be sure to obtain the help of professional translators. Make certain the translators know the colloquial language of your targeted country. As you have learned in this book, a knowledge of, say, Spanish does not mean the same Spanish translation is appropriate for separate Latin American markets.

6. Later, as you evolve into local advertising, do not make the mistake of many American companies who retain an overseas advertising agency and simply send out copies of their U.S. advertising. It is far better to sit down with the overseas ad agency and explain the philosophy of

your company, go over the sense of the message you are trying to communicate, and then let them translate that message into the local vernacular in both words and images.

For example, in The Parker Pen Company, because our products were both high quality and high priced, we always tried to convey impressions of prestige, giftability, and value. Consequently, our U.S. ad agency once designed a print ad with a picture of a handsome man presenting a gleaming pen set to a beautiful woman while standing in front of a Rolls-Royce auto. We sent it to the Parker distributor in Venezuela who assumed we wanted the same ad used there. Many months later, we found out there were absolutely no Rolls-Royce autos in Venezuela, so the imagery was completely wasted. When we asked how best to convey our message to the Venezuelan public, the local advertising agency recommended hiring a popular romantic film star from that country and having him present our pen set to a beautiful woman. Sales improved almost overnight.

7. Pay special attention to product names. As you have read in this chapter, coined or contrived brand names can have surprising meanings when crossing over to another language.

8. Remember, too, that different colors communicate different messages. Red is regarded as an "old" color in England, yet in Japan the combination of red and white is widely regarded as appropriate for happy and pleasant occasions. White is right for brides in the United States but not in India, where red or yellow is used. In Japan, white is the color for both death and weddings because it symbolizes rebirth. Purple is the color for death in Brazil and Mexico. And so it goes.

Having provided this brief assortment of advice, which may tend to portray international sales as problematic, I still strongly encourage American businesspeople to consider international sales. The U.S. Department of Commerce estimates that some 200,000 American medium- and small-size businesses are capable of exporting but are not doing so. The reason? Fear of the unknown. Fear of dealing in strange currencies; fear of new rules for shipping, packaging, and paperwork involved with exports; and fear of having to deal with people who don't speak English. Yet it has been proven over and over through the decades that American companies that become involved in exporting tend to grow faster and make more profits than companies that do not. And finally, as just explained, there is a great deal of support and assistance available for any company wishing to expand its field of operations. For more information on this subject, I would refer you to my book *Do's and Taboos of International Trade: A Small Business Primer,* Revised Edition (Wiley, 1994).

9

Foods and Dining

One of my sales managers, Luis M., was born, raised, and educated in Ecuador. To broaden his experience, I took him to Japan to study our business there. It was his first visit to that Asian country, so one evening, to acquaint him with the local customs, I took him to a sushi bar. When our food came, he looked at his plate, poked at the raw fish with his fork, and asked, "What is this?" I explained it was a Japanese delicacy called sushi. After a moment's reflection, Luis replied, "In my country we would call this bait."

Travel anywhere outside the United States and you'll surely want to explore cosmopolitan restaurants and experiment with the local cuisine. Businesspeople, especially, find themselves hosting, or being hosted by, their international counterparts at restaurants with new and exotic decor. But the strange surroundings are just the beginning. The menu is likely to look like a computer printout gone amok. And, even when deciphered, the foods will hardly resemble McDonald's.

Some of the best stories brought back to the United States by international travelers involve strange-looking dishes of food that some international host insisted on ordering in your honor. Some examples are bear's paw soup in China, reindeer

International cuisine

tongue in Sweden, chocolate-coated ants in Mexico, sheep's eyeballs in Saudi Arabia, and (shades of the *Indiana Jones* movies) . . . yes, monkey brains in Southeast Asia.

Following are more stories about food and dining that reinforce the fact that sustenance in the global village is, truly, more a strange smorgasbord than a simple soup-and-sandwich.

Wacky Meals

A large multinational corporation located in Hartford, Connecticut, once hosted a delegation of visiting Chinese businesspeople. Wishing to entertain them at a dinner in proper Asian fashion, the Americans ordered large circular tables with turntables in the middle, as is common in China. They also placed chopsticks at each place, along with fortune cookies.

The first indication of trouble came when the group sat down: the Americans immediately picked up the chopsticks, and the Chinese picked up forks. Then, unaware that fortune cookies were unknown in China (they were actually invented by a California noodle maker in 1912), the Americans watched while several of the Chinese ate the cookies and, without realizing it, sat for several moments with the paper slips hanging loosely from their lips.

+

Cal Rabas, an automotive engineer from Wisconsin, once traveled to northern Mexico to visit a supplier of parts for his company. During the visit, his Mexican hosts took Cal and his colleagues to a very fancy local restaurant. The menu was both new and elaborate for the Americans, and when it was time for dessert, the waiter placed a bowl of brown liquid in front of Cal. Floating on top of the liquid were a number of small pieces of pastry. Not wishing to offend his hosts, Cal dutifully tried one of the pieces, found it tasty, and so ate the remainder. Later, as they were being driven back to their hotel, their translator said, "Wow, Cal. You surely are a good eater. Remember that dessert you ate? That was intended for all six of us!"

+

An American woman visiting Athens decided to order breakfast at an outdoor restaurant. She asked for scrambled eggs, and the waiter repeated, "Yes, yes. Of course. Scrambly ags." A short time later, he returned with two fried eggs, sunny-side up. "No, no," she said, "I ordered them scrambled." The waiter nodded and took the eggs back to the kitchen. However, once again he returned with two fried eggs. This time the woman said slowly, but with emphasis, "No, no, scrambled, like this . . ." and made a distinct, quick stirring motion with her hands. Minutes later, the waiter returned bearing two fried eggs; but just before presenting them, he made two perfect pirouettes with his body and then set the plate in front of her with a satisfied grin.

✝

The wife of a businessman from Bogotá, Colombia, agreed to accompany her husband on a business trip to New York City. This would be the woman's first visit to America, and she was concerned and nervous because she spoke only a few words of English and would be unaccompanied during the daytime hours. "What will I do about ordering food in a restaurant?" she asked her husband. "Well," he responded, "what would you like to eat?" When she explained that she probably would want to order a hamburger, french fries, and a soda, her husband patiently sounded out the proper English words. On the first day the plan worked beautifully. The woman entered a restaurant in New York, sat down, and when the waiter attended her, she said slowly, "Hamburger . . . french fries . . . and a soda." This formula also worked on the second day, and the third. That evening she confessed to her husband that she was tiring of the same menu every day. So he asked her what she would like to order instead. She replied, "An omelet, toast, and coffee." Once again, the husband coached her with the appropriate English words. At noon, the woman entered a restaurant, sat down, and when the waitress asked for her order, dutifully repeated, "Omelet . . . toast . . . and coffee." The waitress responded with, "Whole wheat, white, or rye?" Bewildered, the Latin woman looked blankly at the waitress . . . and then simply said: "Hamburger, french fries, and a soda."

✝

Frank Plencner, former director of tourism for the state of Arizona, tells about one occasion when he was required to host four important government officials from the People's Republic of China. As it happened, their visit extended over the Thanksgiving holiday. Frank and his wife decided to invite the visitors to their home for a traditional Thanksgiving dinner. The guests were, of course, fascinated by the decorations, and none had ever seen or eaten roast turkey. The mashed potatoes, stuffing, yams, and cranberries were also new. Frank happened to notice one guest being handed the gravy: the Chinese man looked around, somewhat confused, and then proceeded to drink the entire boat of gravy!

✝

Speaking of Thanksgiving, one unthinking American asked his British visitor, "How do you celebrate Thanksgiving in your country?" The Britisher paused for a moment, smiled, and replied dryly, "I suppose you could say in Britain we celebrate Thanksgiving on the Fourth of July."

✝

In both France and England, it is customary and acceptable for patrons to bring their pet dogs into restaurants or pubs. In addition, staff from the restaurant will often bring the pets tidbits from the kitchen or even take them into the kitchen for a treat. A travel agent from Albany, New York, told me that she was once hired to accompany a French couple on a privately directed tour of Asia. They insisted on taking their dog, a French poodle, along on the trip. In one Asian country, the three people—plus the poodle—dined at a local restaurant. When the waiter, using gestures, indicated that he would take the dog into the kitchen, the couple readily agreed. Some time later, the waiter returned with a large covered platter, lifted the lid, and revealed the dog—fully cooked!

✝

The national drink in Peru is known as Pisco Sour. It is a lime-colored drink that tastes like a margarita but carries a much more powerful punch. The head of the American Chamber of Commerce in Lima related to me that on one occasion, a visiting American businessman was observed downing glass after glass of Pisco Sour because of its seemingly benign taste. At the end of the meal, hearing music coming from the nearby ballroom, the inebriated businessman weaved his way into the room and headed for a distinguished person dressed in a long red robe with attractive white hair. Attempting to be suave, he asked, "Would you care to dance?" The person looked at him and replied stiffly, "In the first place they are playing the Peruvian national anthem . . . and secondly, I am the archbishop of Lima."

✝

"Would you care to dance?"

In the Far East, eating the meat from dogs is common. My wife and I once hosted a visitor from Hong Kong, and in true American style, we started the barbecue grill and loaded it with hamburger patties and hot dogs. When we offered our visitor the latter, he admitted he was unfamiliar with that particular item and asked what it was called. "We call it a 'hot dog,'" we explained. Considering that for a moment, he replied, "We eat dog in my country . . . but not *that* part!"

Funny Eating Techniques

Mr. Satish was a Pakistani hired by a large American consumer goods company to manage its factory in Pakistan. To acquaint him with their manufacturing methods, they invited him to the home offices in the United States. Satish had never traveled outside of Pakistan, so everything about America was new for him.

On the first morning of the visit, they toured the facilities, and after a time Satish's American host, Larry, asked if he would like to take a break for coffee or tea. Satish replied that he would, indeed, enjoy a cup of tea. In the company cafeteria the two men went to the coffee bar where Larry gave Mr. Satish a cup and a tea bag. Satish promptly tore the tea bag open and put the leaves in his cup. "No, no," Larry interrupted. "Here we put the whole bag in the cup and then pour hot water over it." "Oh, I'm sorry if I embarrassed you," Satish apologized. "Such wonderful things you have here in America."

They then proceeded to sit at a table where Larry asked if Satish would like some sugar. When he nodded yes, Larry gave him the sugar bowl containing paper packets of sugar. Later, Larry commented: "I could almost see the light bulb of comprehension lighting up in Satish's head. He looked at the paper packets of sugar and then plopped two of them directly into the tea, saying, 'You surely do have wonderful things here in America.'"

┼

A woman in Rockford, Illinois, lived near a community college and enjoyed inviting visiting international students to spend weekends in her home so they could learn how Americans lived. On one of these occasions, she invited a young man from Iceland to stay with her and her family. As she helped him unpack, she noticed that in his suitcase he had a collection of a dozen or more *table forks*—each one different from the next. Curious, she asked, "I hope you don't mind my asking, but why do you have all those different forks?" The young man explained that during his time in the United States he was often invited into private homes for dinner. "And," he said, "it's very strange. The hostess always cooks a nice meal, and toward the end of the meal she'll say, 'Keep your fork.' So I do."

†

A U.S. company in South Carolina once hosted a group of Japanese businesspeople. At dinner one evening, the chief host, an American, noticed that one of the prominent Japanese visitors did not look well. When he inquired, the Japanese gentleman confessed that he was suffering from a slight upset stomach. The American searched and found two Alka-Seltzer tablets and gave them to the guest, saying, "Here . . . take these. They will help settle your stomach." Returning to his chair some distance away, he happened to look back and observe, with horror, that the Japanese man was putting the tablets directly into his mouth rather than dropping them in a glass of water. Before the American could get the other's attention, he saw that the Japanese man's first reaction was that the tablets tasted dry and bitter . . . so he reached for his glass of water and started drinking. Before he could return to rescue his guest, a large quantity of white foam started streaming from his mouth!

†

Peace Corps volunteer Kiki Clark was advised that in her little village in Ethiopia it was customary to eat most meals with one's fingers. After one especially messy dinner, and since nap-

kins were not available, Kiki leaned over to her Ethiopian
male friend and jokingly asked: "Can I rub my hands on your
pants?" He burst into laughter and explained that in Ethiopia,
the word "pants" referred to a person's underwear.

✝

The variety of American restaurants can create confusion for
visitors from overseas. The program director at the Chicago
International Visitor's Center told me that one young international visitor who knew a smattering of English entered a
cafeteria in the Windy City, sat down, and waited to be served.
A staff member finally told him that this was a "self-serve"
restaurant. So the visitor got up, went into the kitchen, and
started to cook himself a meal.

✝

Ian Kerr, a distinguished British businessman, recalls visiting a midwestern motel with attached restaurant. He entered the restaurant and had his evening meal. At the conclusion, his waitress politely asked, "Coffee?" "Yes," he nodded, "but I'd like a demitasse, please." Without missing a beat, the waitress responded, "Oh, I'm afraid all we have is Sanka."

✝

It is said that one definition of the word "etiquette" is "to never embarrass one's guest in any way." David Ryan, an engaging young man who has traveled to many remote parts of the world, related a perfect example of that rule to me. One of his trips took him to the country of Laos, where he visited a college friend whose father also happened to be the U.S. ambassador to that country. At a dinner in honor of a Laotian chieftain, David noticed that finger bowls containing perfumed water were discreetly placed at each table setting. David and others happened to be watching as the chief studied the small bowl, picked it up with his two hands, and drank the full contents. The other guests sat in embarrassed silence . . . until the ambassador coolly took his finger bowl in both hands and slowly drank the water. Following his example, all the others at the table did exactly the same. Conversation resumed, and the dinner was completed without a hitch. Later that evening, the son of the diplomat told David, "I've never been so proud of my father as I was this evening."

✝

An enterprising restaurateur in Hong Kong once advertised "all you can eat" . . . but then provided his patrons with only one chopstick.

How and When to Use Humor

Let's start with an easy piece of advice: When traveling anywhere overseas, whether for business or pleasure, it would probably not be a good idea to try your hand at humor by starting a food fight at the dinner table. However, *the dinner table is a remarkably fine place to relax, enjoy another person's company, and build those all-important new relationships.* Therefore, what better place to cautiously explore, in a figurative sense, the ticklish spots of your companions? This could be a comfortable setting in which to launch into a discussion that could be titled "Humor around the World." What a wonderful opportunity to learn how one culture views the humor quotient of surrounding cultures.

More Advice

In a turn of the tables, lest you conclude that only in America do we serve "sensible" food, here is a list of dishes your international guests may find strange—even repulsive—when they sit down at an American dinner table:

Pumpkin and pecan pies
Grits
Marshmallows
Catsup
White (preservative-filled) bread
Sweet potatoes
Roast turkey
Very rare beef

And the food many visitors consider the most distasteful? Corn on the cob. The reason that summertime American favorite is on the blacklist is because throughout Europe, and in many other regions, corn on the cob is served only to *animals.* So—what do we do? We tell our international guests that we

An American tradition . . . corn on the cob.

are going to have a cookout, we put water on to boil, and we dump in ear after ear of (to their minds) "animal food." We then lather the ears with melted butter, apply excessive amounts of salt and pepper, and start champing away with all the vigor of an out-of-control typewriter. When we stop for a breather and look up at our guests, what they see are people with butter dripping down their chins and pieces of corn stuck between their teeth. We can't blame them for thinking: "First he serves me animal food . . . and then he *looks like an animal* when he eats it!"

The question nearly every American traveler asks regarding strange, unfamiliar foods overseas is this: "What should I do when confronted with some weird-looking dish? Must I eat it, or can I refuse?" The answer lies in these facts:

- First, you are probably the guest of honor. Your hosts are paying you a compliment by serving special foods.
- Second, the food they are offering is very likely a local delicacy—one that the people in that country have been eating for decades, maybe even for centuries, and it hasn't harmed them.
- Third, consider what your reaction would be if you offered your international guest roast turkey or a thick beef steak, and they pushed it away.

Therefore, the best advice is to at least try it. And here are some tricks to employ: Cut it up into small pieces. Eat it quickly. Pretend it's chicken or some other familiar food. You don't have to eat it all (in fact, if you do, they may offer you more!), but at least try to be gracious enough to try it.

Another common question is this: "What should I do if I don't drink alcohol and my host offers me a cocktail or wine?" The answer is simple: politely decline. Ask for fruit juice or soda. If you host persists or shows surprise, just explain that you don't drink alcohol, but you certainly don't mind if others do. Another trick is to take your host aside early in your socializing and explain that you don't drink alcohol but are perfectly comfortable if and when others do. From that point on, your host will probably intercede and discreetly ensure you are served nonalcoholic beverages. As for participating in toasts where wine is served, you do not have to drink the wine—just bring the glass up to your lips and pretend to sip.

10

Toasts

In Spain, when toasting, the phrase *chin-chin* is often used. In Japan, however, *chin-chin* is a term that means a small boy's penis. A Japanese businessman told me he was unaware of this Spanish toasting phrase, so he was rather startled when his Spanish host stood at dinner, raised his glass, and said *"chin-chin."* The Japanese man thought to himself, "Well, if he wants to toast my pee-pee, that's OK with me."

Toasting is a lost art in America. We do it, perhaps, on New Year's Eve, and, if you are happen to be the best man at a wedding, you are obligated to offer a formal toast to the glowing bride and groom. Otherwise—no big deal. However, when you travel abroad, toasting is more common and sometimes more complicated, as you will learn from the stories that follow.

Incidentally, the tradition of raising a glass of spirits to someone's health began with the ancient Greeks. It was the Romans who caused that gesture to be called a "toast." It seems they discovered that adding a piece of toast to a glass of inferior wine made it mellower.

Wittily Worldly Toasts

A young woman from my hometown travels to Houston to teach English to people from South America and the Middle East who come to Texas to learn the oil business. At the conclusion of one of her courses, one of her students, a Middle Eastern gentleman, asked if he might take her out for dinner, "to celebrate the conclusion of the course and to practice my new English." The teacher thought that would be acceptable and they agreed on a date and time.

On the appointed evening, the Middle Easterner arrived in front of her apartment in a huge stretch limousine. He then took her to the finest restaurant in Houston. He ordered the meal in perfect French! He ordered a bottle of expensive French wine, poured two glasses, held his glass up to the candlelight, looked directly into the eyes of the young woman, and said, "Well . . . up yours!"

What he had meant to say, of course, was, "Bottoms up!" After hearing this story, I asked the woman, "What was your reaction? What did you do?" She replied, "I gave him 'the finger.' So he learned that that night, too."

＋

In the spring of 1976, I was part of a group of fifteen businesspeople from the Middle West granted permits to visit the People's Republic of China. This was somewhat unprecedented because then President Richard Nixon had opened the doors to China only a few short years earlier, and until that point only specialists had been permitted entry into that gigantic enigma known as mainland China. We represented an assortment of different companies—banks, manufacturers, agricultural firms, and so on. At this early stage in the thawing of the Sino-American relationship, the Chinese were not accustomed to hosting Americans, and the result was that both sides regarded the other with cautious curiosity.

The U.S. State Department advised us that we would be hosted at numerous elaborate dinners and, when possible, we

"Well . . . up yours."

should reciprocate. We were also informed that it was the custom in China for one representative of each group to toast the other. At the first dinner we attended, our group leader said to me, "OK. We want to impress the Chinese, so at this dinner I want you to deliver our toast in Chinese." "But I don't speak Chinese," I protested. "How can I do that?" He replied, "We have it all written out here phonetically, so just memorize these phrases." I assured him I would certainly try, but out of curiosity, I asked, "What am I saying?" He said, "You are saying 'Thank you very much for this lovely dinner. I have eaten so much I have to loosen my belt.'" Inwardly, I couldn't understand why they had chosen that particular message, but I was assured it was proper and appropriate. So I spent the better part of a day memorizing the sounds they had put to paper.

That evening, I rose and delivered my toast. I could see our Chinese hosts were surprised. Knowing that Chinese is a "tonal" language—meaning inflections are both subtle and important—I later in the evening approached a U.S. official who was bilingual and asked, "Was my toast OK?" He said, "Well, you got through the first part all right, 'Thank you very much for the lovely dinner . . . ,' but then you said something like, '. . . and the girth of the donkey's saddle is loose.'"

✝

Hernando Cardenas, of Bogotá, Colombia, was Parker Pen's distributor for that country, and at least once a year he would come to our headquarters in Wisconsin for a review of business plans. One evening, during dinner at a local restaurant with a group of our executives, he turned to me and, in Spanish, said, "This is such a memorable and enjoyable evening, I would like to propose a toast to our group. Would that be permitted?" When I quickly assured him it would be very appropriate, he added, "This is an old Colombian toast that I will try to translate into English." I urged him to proceed. To get the group's attention, he stood and raised his glass. At this particular moment, there happened to be a hush throughout the restaurant, so all the other patrons heard exactly what followed. "I should like to make a toast," Hernando declared with great ceremony. "To all of you! Today has been a marvelous day! May I say that this is the most fun I have ever had—dressed!" After a moment's silence, the entire restaurant broke out in delighted laughter and applause. Turning to me with a surprised look, Hernando asked, "Did I say that OK?" "Yes, of course," I replied. "In fact, I don't know how you possibly could have been more descriptive."

✝

A Venezuelan businessman once related to me that he had been in the United States for only a few months, struggling to learn English, when he was invited to an American home for dinner. Near the end of the meal, he decided it would be gracious to present a toast of thanks to his hosts. He stood, apologized for his poor English, and slowly and haltingly said the following: "Thank you . . . for this . . . fine . . . dinner. Thank

you . . . for the . . . good . . . wine. But . . . most . . . of all . . . thank
you . . . for . . . your . . . friendshit."

Generally Funny Toasts

The following is a toast on "How to Enjoy Life." I have been
told it is both an old German and an ancient Chinese toast, but
I have been unable to confirm it comes from both cultures. Suffice it to say, its origins are apparently old, even though some
of the examples used here have been modernized.

> A toast on how to enjoy life:
> To enjoy life for one hour . . . get drunk.
> To enjoy life for one day . . . play golf.
> To enjoy life for one week . . . kill a pig (so that you'll have
>   plenty of food.)
> To enjoy life for one month . . . get married!
> To enjoy life for one year . . . inherit a million dollars.
> But! To enjoy life for a *lifetime* . . . have good friends!

✝

The following is a very short toast from the Swedish poet/
architect Piet Hein:

> Live while you have life to live.
> Love while you have love to give.

✝

This toast is particularly suited for weddings, anniversaries,
or retirements, where you wish to toast a husband and wife.
(Note: With this toast, it is important to use the timing suggested in parentheses.)

> Ladies and gentlemen, I would like to propose a toast to John
> and Joan. (Pause to get everyone's attention.) Now . . . this is
> a rather unusual, even unconventional, toast, so I would ask

you to bear with me. (Long pause . . . for as much silence as possible.)

This is a toast . . . (solemnly) . . . to *lying!* . . . *stealing!* . . . and . . . *cheating!* (It is important to allow for a pause here because, frankly, many of those attending will think perhaps you have had too much to drink! Then continue.)

To John and Joan. May you *lie* in each other's arms and comfort one another for many years to come.

And may you *steal* away from time to time and remember the love and friendship that is present in this room tonight.

And, finally, may you both *cheat* Father Time and live and love one another for a hundred more years!

Note: At this point, the audience will be so surprised and pleased that you are not drunk, they will very likely applaud with great approval.

✝

Here are several old Irish toasts:

- May you have food and raiment,
  A soft pillow for your head,
  May you be forty years in heaven
  Before the devil knows you're dead!

- May you live to be
  A hundred years,
  With one extra year to repent.

- May you have warm words
  On a cold evening,
  A full moon on a dark night,
  And the road downhill all the way to your door.

- May those who love us, love us;
  And those that don't love us,
  May God turn their hearts;
  And if He doesn't turn their hearts,

May He turn their ankles,
So we'll know them by their limping.

✝

Here's to the bee—the busy soul;
He has no time for birth control.
That's why it is, in times like these,
We have so many sons of bees!

✝

Harry Franke is a prominent attorney in Milwaukee, a world
traveler, and the perennial master of ceremonies at major social functions throughout Wisconsin. He has a favorite toast
that is suitable any place in the world because it sounds bril-
liant, has something for everyone, but is absolutely incomprehensible. With thanks to Harry, here it is. (It's best when read
aloud.)

Dearly beloved,
We are gathered here to the last syllable of recorded time,
And all of our yesterdays spread out before us like
The claws that bite, the jaws that catch.
Render unto Caesar the things that are Caesar's
By the shining big sea water.
Aye, that is the question:
Whether we the aforementioned
Wondering at this brief token of your esteem
Ask not what you can do for your country
Like the wanton lute who struts and frets his hour upon the
    stage
And then is heard no more.
Out, out, brief spots,
Life is but a walking shadow.
A poor player who struts and frets his hour upon the stage,
And then is heard no more.
Once more into the breach, dear friend,
And screw thy courage to the sticking point.

That this government of the people, by the people, and for
   the people
Shall not be rent asunder.
For the moon never beams without bringing me dreams of a
Ich weiß nicht, was es bedeuten soll.
There once was a hermit named Dave
Tonight's the night, if she dies, she dies
You're a better man than I am, Hillary Clinton!

☦

Finally, if toasts should be brief, appropriate, and memorable, here is a paradigm provided by Alan Fredericks, editor of *Travel* magazine. Fredericks was visiting in China and attended a large formal dinner hosted by the Chinese. At the end of the long evening, the Chinese host stood and raised his glass to the audience and said in English: "Thank you for coming. Now go home!"

How and When to Use Humor

Generally, the tone and message of, say, an after-dinner toast should be as follows: gracious, complimentary, sincere, and, above all, short. You'll note that "humorous" is not included. The reason is because if your choice of humor should fall flat, so will the entire toast. And the whole purpose of rising and raising your glass in tribute to some person or occasion is to leave those attending with a memory of an enjoyable and convivial evening together . . . not of a joke that failed. Of course, your toast can be mildly amusing, but the final sentence or two should be designed to evoke murmurs of approval and agreement from all those around you because of your remarkably sensitive and sentimental insight. So, as evidenced in this chapter, develop a safe repertoire of all-purpose toasts, memorize or carry them with you when traveling abroad, and inject humor only when you have practiced and tested it previously on diverse audiences. This latter point is critical: even professional comedians will try out their stories before inserting them in their main routines. Therefore, *when toasting or in any public speaking circumstance, avoid the spur-of-the-moment decision to ad lib what seems to be at that particular moment a great punch line.*

More Advice

My first lesson in international toasting occurred in 1968 in Hong Kong. I was the guest of honor at an elaborate Chinese dinner, attended by a group of influential local businesspeople. It was a typical, first-rate Chinese multicourse meal: we sat at a large round table with a "lazy Susan" turntable in the middle. The specially printed menu indicated at least eight separate courses, with each successive course set out on the rotating turntable and then removed for the next serving. About halfway through the evening, my host nudged me gently and said, "Now would be a good time." "Now?" I asked. "What do you mean 'now'?" He whispered, "Now would be a good time to make your toast." I later learned that the shark's fin soup was being served, making this the apex of the meal and the traditional time for toasts to be made. Naturally, I fumbled and stuttered and generally left a terrible impression.

My second misadventure occurred in Stockholm. I was invited to the home of our distributor for Sweden, an older and very distinguished gentleman. Ten of us were seated around the dinner table. The host turned to me and said in a low voice: "Since you are seated at my left, you are expected to make a toast and you must try to say something about each person at the table." To this day, I'm not certain if this was an old Swedish custom or if he was pulling my leg. I do remember that my stomach tightened and my mind went blank. I rose, did my best, sat down, and vowed to learn more about toasting. As the dinner progressed, my host instructed me in performing the proper "Skoal!" Swedish style: "Look someone directly in the eyes, lift your glass upward from the seventh button down on your waistcoat up to your eye level, drink, then lower the glass back down." (I found out later that was the proper protocol practiced by the older generation in Sweden.) But my host also warned me, "Never Skoal the hostess if she has less than six guests. That is because with less than six, she will probably prepare and serve the dinner herself, and too many Skoals will get her drunk." He went on to explain, "With more than six guests, the hostess is expected to have help cooking and serving the dinner, so it's permitted to Skoal her."

Here are more tips to prepare you for toasting around the world:

1. Remember, a toast can be a marvelous moment to express special sentiments that might normally sound hollow during a business meeting.
2. Be prepared. Collect a repertoire of short toasts. Books filled with a variety of toasts are available at your local library. A safe recourse is to compliment your hosts on the long and glorious history of their country and thank them for their friendship and warm hospitality; if your visit is on business, you can comment on your hope for a long and mutually satisfactory relationship, compliment the meal, and so on.
3. Normally, the host makes the first toast and the guest responds. If your host shows no sign of rising for a toast, proper protocol suggests you quietly request permission to offer one.
4. Keep it short. Long-winded toasts tend to be boring.
5. Make eye contact with everyone, but especially the chief host and hostess (or honored guest).
6. If you don't drink alcohol, don't worry about being required to drink the wine. Just pretend to take a sip.
7. Most countries have one-word toasts. Throughout Scandinavia, the word used most commonly when toasting is *skoal* (rhymes with "coal"). Throughout most of Latin America, it is *salud* (sah-lood), which means "health." In

German-speaking countries, the word is *prost* (rhymes with "roast"). In France, the word is *santé* (sahn-TAY, meaning "health"). And in most of Asia the word is *kan-pie* (kahn-pye, or sometimes pronounced kahn-bye), which means "bottoms up."

11

Travel Talk

I once phoned the desk clerk in an Indonesian hotel to leave a wake-up call. The clerk said, "Oh, we've installed alarm clocks in every room for that purpose." "But what happens if it doesn't work?" I asked. After a pause he replied, "Just call me."

World travel is glamorous, right? Wrong. Not always. Just talk to those veteran business travelers who must travel the globe for a livelihood. One friend traveled abroad for more than six months of each year. After one long absence he returned home, retired to bed with his wife, only to have her awaken in the middle of the night screaming that there was a strange man in bed with her!

Another bromide among seasoned travelers is this: "I think I'm going to ask my boss if I can go off salary and go on to mileage. I think I'll make more money that way."

Every veteran international businessperson has favorite stories to tell about traveling. Here are just two of my own.

✝

I traveled for weeks on end with Stewart S. throughout Latin America, which means, of course, spending many evenings and airplane rides together. Suffice it to say, on trips like that you get to know each other well. During one of our many conversations, I happened to comment that one of my personal quirks was that I could not tolerate sleeping in a room where someone else was snoring. "You won't ever have to worry about me," Stewart assured me. "I don't snore. I know it for a fact."

Several months later, he was in the United States attending a national sales meeting being held at the former Playboy Club at Lake Geneva, Wisconsin. One evening, as the hour turned late, he said to me: "You have a long drive back home, and it's late, so why don't you stay here for the night? I have a large room and the couch turns into a daybed. And—by the way—I know how you feel about sharing a room with someone who might snore. But don't worry! I can guarantee that I don't snore." So I agreed to stay the night.

As I got settled into my daybed, Stewart's head no sooner hit the pillow than he started snoring with such a loud, rasping rattle that the drapes shook. I tried placing the pillow over my head, but I could still hear Stewart. Then I tried stuffing bits and pieces of torn newspaper in my ears, but every time I turned over the paper crunched and crackled like guns going off inside my ears. Finally, I rolled the sheets and blankets into my thin mattress and tiptoed quietly into the bathroom. I experimented and found that if I placed my head directly beneath the sink, I could just fit. I closed the door, turned out the lights . . . and was rewarded with blessed silence. As I was falling off to sleep, I suddenly wondered if there would be enough ventilation in that bathroom to keep me alive. I could just see the headlines in our small local newspaper: LOCAL BUSINESSMAN SUFFOCATES AT PLAYBOY CLUB WHILE SHARING ROOM WITH ASSOCIATE.

Nevertheless, I made it through the night and early the next morning, very quietly—so as not to disturb Stewart—crept back into the room. As I gathered my toilet articles and started to return to the bathroom, Stewart awakened. "Well, now," he said, "did I snore last night?" I decided that since he was unaware of his snoring, there was no need to trouble him. There-

fore I lied and said, "No, Stewart. Everything was fine." Whereupon he said, somewhat ruffled, "Well, that's good . . . but you
sure make a helluva lot of noise. You kept me awake for half
the night!"

╋

On another occasion, I was traveling in the Middle East with
a colleague, Richard Brewer, an American who resided in
Australia. We had been to Kuwait and Iran and now were in
Baghdad, in Iraq. At that time (mid-1970s), relationships between the United States and Iraq were strained, but the Iraqi
government had allocated several hundred thousand dollars
for the purchase of writing instruments and we were there to
try to land the order. On the evening of our arrival, our hotel
clerk informed us he had no record of our reservations. After
we "tipped" him ten dollars, he discovered he had one room
available. Once in the room we found that, first, the toilet was
backed up, and second, there was no running water. Furthermore, there was no restaurant open and we had missed dinner.
Today, I can still vividly picture us sitting on our suitcases, a
bed between us serving as a table, feasting on a tin of fine
caviar we had brought from Iran and washing it down with
Scotch whisky. (Needless to say, I didn't hear if Brewer snored
or not that night.)

It took us a full week to negotiate our business in Baghdad,
with long periods of cooling our heels. We had been warned to
carefully reconfirm our departure flight arrangements, and so
we did that, not once but three times, including a special trip
to the airport just to reconfirm there as well. When the time
came to depart, I approached the ticket counter at the airport
and was told very brusquely that I had failed to reconfirm and
therefore there was no seat available for me. I protested but
was dismissed. Brewer had already been processed and had
boarded the plane, so I was stranded. There were no other
flights departing that day, my visa for Iraq had expired, all the
hotels were filled, and my only option was to try to hire a car
and driver to take me across Syria (for which I had no visa)

and on to Beirut. Considering all this, I made a terrible mistake! I swore. The ticket agent thought I was swearing at *him!* He picked up my air ticket and passport and threw them across the room. With my stomach muscles beginning to spasm and sweat starting to stream, I retreated to a corner to consider my alternatives. There was only one: I returned to the counter and apologized profusely. No, I didn't apologize . . . I groveled. I watched as the plane filled with passengers and started its engines while the ground crew prepared to remove the stairway. At that last moment, the clerk finally motioned me forward, handed me my passport and ticket, and said, rudely: "Go!"

Later that day, after our safe arrival in Amman, Jordan, friends there informed me what had probably happened. They speculated that the Iraqi airline was probably holding a seat open in case, at the last moment, some high-level government official decided to travel that day . . . and I just happened to be the unlucky victim.

Moral: Not *all* international travel is glamorous.

Travel Titters

For international visitors to the United States, our choice of words and terms for ordinary, everyday places and events must sometimes be confounding. For example, consider a visit to any major U.S. airport. When driving into the airport, people are greeted by large overhead signs offering two choices: "Arrivals" or "Departures." Since they are "arriving," that must be the proper choice, right? Wrong. They learn that they are, indeed, "arriving" in order to "depart" and that "arrivals" refers to people arriving on airplanes. But they can't be blamed for thinking: "But passengers are arriving on airplanes, and then departing from those planes to enter the terminal . . . so which is correct?"

After sorting out that dilemma, and when checking in at a ticket counter, people are instructed to proceed to "gate such-and-such." When they arrive at that "gate" . . . there is no gate.

There is no swinging bar, or half-door, or any semblance of a "gate." What is there is a door. After a period of waiting, passengers are then instructed to get on the airplane. As comedian George Carlin comments: "I don't know about you, but I'd rather get *in* the airplane than on it." Later, at the conclusion of the flight, the flight attendant often announces: "Thank you for flying (name) airlines, and we hope you will have a pleasant journey to your final destination." After one of these announcements, a passenger next to me turned and said: "Well . . . I don't know about you, but I'm not *ready* to travel to my final destination just yet."

This story falls under the category "weird people you meet when traveling." A young businesswoman named Marjorie was in the International Terminal of O'Hare Airport in Chicago waiting for her flight overseas. Seeing that she had some extra time before the departure of her flight, she visited the refreshment counter and purchased a soft drink and candy bar. She then turned and approached a nearby table. A gentleman (obviously not American) was seated, but in situations like this, sharing tables is both common and accepted, so she placed her soda on the table, placed her coat on the back of her chair, and sat down. She tore the wrapper off the candy bar and took a sip from the soda. To her amazement, and without saying a word, the man reached over, broke off a piece of the candy bar, and ate it. She said nothing, pulled the bar back to her side, broke off a wedge of the candy, and ate it. After a pause, once again the man reached over, broke off another piece, and swallowed it. This continued—back and forth—until the candy was gone. Not a word was said, and Marjorie just shrugged it off as an innocent but somewhat upsetting incident. Later, after boarding her plane and becoming settled in her seat, she opened her purse . . . and was stunned to see *her* candy bar sitting there, untouched.

Moral: Sometimes *we* are the weird "foreigners."

Ethiopia is not exactly a magnet for tourism. As a result, travel stories from that country are not plentiful. However, Kiki Clark, the dedicated Peace Corps volunteer referred to earlier in this book, provided this peek at life there:

> We play a game here that we call "Fortunately/Unfortunately," which helps provide humor during challenging times. Here are three examples:
> - Fortunately, we have hot water for showers. Unfortunately, it comes out as only a slight dribble.
> - Fortunately, on this hot bus we are sitting next to a window. Unfortunately, we aren't allowed to open the windows.
> - Fortunately, we have beds. Unfortunately, we also have bed bugs.

I mentioned earlier that when AFS Intercultural Programs chooses students for international exchange programs, one of the characteristics they seek in young people is a good sense of humor. We should add the Peace Corps to that list . . . and tip our hats to wonderful young people like Kiki Clark.

✝

When we Americans travel overseas we automatically say, "Hello. How are you?" when we meet people. Kirsten Olsen is the wife of a Danish businessman, and she and her husband travel frequently to the United States. Kirsten speaks and writes four languages (Danish, English, German, and French). "One thing that troubles me about American English," Kirsten says, "is that when people greet me they say, 'Hello, how are you?' We don't say that in Danish. In fact, we have no equivalent, so we don't know how to respond." As cross-cultural trainer Dr. Joan Rea adds, "The irony is that when Americans ask 'How are you?' we really *don't want to know!* For example, in America if you say to the checkout person at the supermarket, 'How are you?' and they stop everything to respond, 'Well, my dog is sick, and my mother-in-law's gallbladder is bothering her, and so on,' you'd think they were crazy."

✝

Johnson Wax cross-cultural trainer Tom Newman was visiting the city of Cork, in the south of Ireland. Searching for an auto route out of the city, he stopped and asked an elderly Irishman for advice. The local man said: "Turn the car around, go down to the corner and turn right, then go straight into the center of the city. Then when you get there, ask someone where the road is, because I don't know where it is."

✝

This sign was affixed to a telephone in Japan: "If phone rings, please answer."

Funny Travel Trick Number One

My brother broke his leg in a skiing accident and, even with a full leg cast, still managed to travel overseas on business. He would request a bulkhead seat because of the extra space, but even that could be uncomfortable, especially if he was stuck in the middle seat on an overnight flight. He confided that he found a solution that always worked. Before the plane took off, he would turn to the person sitting next to him and merely say: "Pardon me. (Then he would point to the seat pocket in front of that passenger.) Are you going to use that airsick bag?" When the person would respond, "No. Why?" my brother would reply, "Because I normally need more than one." Invariably, my brother explained, that person would raise a hand, carry on a whispered conversation with the flight attendant, and be moved to another seat. "You then raise the arm between the seats," my brother would smile, "and you've got two seats all to yourself for the whole night."

"Pardon me, but are you going to use that airsick bag?"

Travel Bathroom Humor

Toilets around the world, and their diversity, could be the entire subject of another book. In England, for instance, they are often referred to as "loos." And one brand of particularly abrasive English toilet paper bears the brand name "Silver Satin," which to your discomfort, feels more like a bar of silver than a bolt of satin. In other English-speaking countries, toilets are often referred to as "WCs" (for "water closets"), and those two letters appear on the door.

We Americans are inclined to use diverse euphemisms as labels for our toilets. We say such things as "the boys' room," or "the rest room," or "the sandbox," or "making a pit stop." But diversity in bathrooms around the world doesn't stop with just labels. Oh, no. In parts of Europe, males may encounter a female attendant inside the bathroom who hands out towels and maintains cleanliness. And they often expect to be tipped.

But my biggest shock came in Saudi Arabia. On my arrival there I was suffering from a touch of diarrhea. Arriving at the offices of our distributor, I immediately inquired about the location of the bathroom. He directed me to the hallway and pointed toward a doorway. I opened the door and stepped inside. There I was greeted by . . . nothing! It appeared to be just an empty room. I thought I had mistakenly entered an unused storeroom. Scanning the room, I spotted a hole in the floor at the far end. Examining it more closely, I discovered in front of the hole what appeared to be two *footprints* embedded in the stone floor. The footprints were splayed away from the hole and had ridges in them—obviously to avoid slipping. By then, the purpose of the hole was quite clear. I was, indeed, in a bathroom. In my dire need, I hastily concluded that if the whole nation of Saudi Arabia could hit that hole, I could, too! Assuming a squatting position, I immediately felt both relieved and far away from home. But another shock was yet to come. As I inspected my surroundings more carefully, I noticed there was no toilet tissue in sight. At first, I assumed it was just my bad luck to be using a toilet without toilet tissue. But then I noted a water pipe descending from the ceiling, ending with a faucet an arm's length away. A small metal pitcher was positioned under the faucet. It took only seconds for me to understand why, throughout the Middle East, the left hand was referred to as the *unclean hand*. In the Middle East, one is cautioned about eating with the left hand, delivering presents or business cards with the left hand, and other such common gestures. Now the reason became fully obvious.

But the Middle East is not the only region to provide surprises when it comes to potties. At the other end of the scale, Japan has in recent years introduced high-tech toilets. More and more American visitors to Japan are reporting that when they go to a bathroom in Japan, especially in large, more modern homes, they are greeted by a complicated panel or keyboard displaying an array of buttons, each bearing a Japanese word or character. One of these discoveries was reported to me by a Midwestern businessman who was traveling in Japan with a high-ranking government official of his state. Here is his story: The two men were being hosted at the home of a prominent Japanese businessman who had significant investments in the government official's state. At the conclusion of dinner, and just before departing to return to their hotel, the official said he had to visit the bathroom. The others waited . . . and waited . . . and waited. Finally, after a long interval, he reappeared, somewhat ruffled, but said nothing to explain his long absence. By this time, the businessman also had to visit the bathroom. As he entered, he was greeted by one of the high-tech toilets just described. He carefully studied each button and each label but had no clue which button flushed the toilet, or what functions the other buttons provided. So he just started pushing one after the other. The first button produced a flushing sound to mask any noise a person might be making. The second button activated a jet of water that shot directly upward! A third button started a blow dryer to dry your bottom, and a fourth button squirted warm water across the room. Another button opened and closed the lid—with separate buttons for men and women. Another button cleaned the toilet with soapy water and—as the executive learned later—a new version is planned that actually scrubs and cleanses your bottom, thus doing away with toilet paper.

At this juncture, however, the bathroom was a total mess. Embarrassed and worried about being absent so long, he merely closed the door and joined the state official. Later, in the limousine taking them to their hotel, the official explained he was delayed because of his encounter with the now-famous buttons, adding, "I had to stay and clean up the whole place." When his partner, the businessman, related his similar experience and stated he merely left the bathroom in its chaotic state, the official moaned, "At least I cleaned it up! Now they'll think we're both guilty!"

✝

A veteran world traveler taught me a trick to use in hotels where the housekeeping service is less than desirable. Here it is: If you want to get the attention of the housekeeper on your floor and make certain your room is kept clean and fresh, here's what to do. As experienced travelers know, many hotels around the world place a strip of paper around the seat of the toilet, often bearing the printed words, "Sanitized for your protection." Most hotel guests, especially Americans, simply tear that strip off and throw it away. My friend advised, "Don't do that. Remove it carefully. Then, each morning, put it *back* around the toilet seat.

"You must do this each morning for, say, two or three mornings. I can almost guarantee that by that time the maid on your floor will stop you and ask, 'Are you the guest in room 406 (or whatever your room number is)?' When you say yes, she will usually reply with something like, 'You Americans are weird,' or 'Are you all right?' or 'Are you feeling OK?' The reason is she thinks you're going to blow up in there . . . and she's going to have to clean everything up!"

+

Nan Hartman, traveling in Peru, asked the manager of a restaurant where she could go to wash her hands. The manager ushered her into a bathroom where some painters happened to be working. When the painters started to leave, the manager stopped them, saying, "That's OK. Don't leave. The lady only wants to wash her hands."

One Man's Travelogue

Larry Greb served thirty years with the S. C. Johnson Wax Company, located in Racine, Wisconsin, and became one of Johnson's most valued international marketing executives. Johnson Wax is a multibillion-dollar manufacturer of consumer goods with over half of its sales outside the United States. Consequently, Greb spent much of his career traveling to far-flung markets for his company. Greb has been a friend of mine since high school days, and for several decades we have shared stories about amusing experiences when traveling abroad. Many of Larry's stories are scattered in this book. Here are a few of his special anecdotes about traveling.

☦

On his first trip to Japan in the late 1950s, Greb flew on Northwest Orient Airlines from Chicago to Anchorage to Tokyo. At that time, many companies like Johnson Wax permitted their executives to fly first class on any flights longer than six hours. It was also a time when the airlines provided exceptionally luxurious service. Greb vividly recalls this first trip:

> On the Anchorage-to-Tokyo leg, after reaching the proper altitude, the purser appeared in a tuxedo and begin serving drinks and hors d'oeuvres. Since I happened to be seated in the very first row, I was served first. The purser brought a large tray of sushi—raw fish, and a Japanese delicacy. When the purser handed me the sushi tray, I assumed the entire tray was for me and so I took it out of his hands. He said nothing and returned to the kitchen. A few minutes later, I suddenly realized the tray was intended for everyone in the first class section. I tried to be nonchalant and called the purser over, saying I'd had enough, and he could take the tray. He returned to the kitchen, refilled the tray with appetizers, and with a firm grip proceeded to pass the sushi to the rest of the passengers. As I left the airplane in Tokyo, I said to him, "Well, you know the saying . . . 'You can take the boy out of the country, but you can't take the country out of the boy.'" The purser broke up in laughter.

☦

Greb also tells about the time he was working with Johnson's German subsidiary in Düsseldorf. On each visit, he would be introduced to new members of the management team there. On one trip he was introduced to the new sales manager, a man named Mr. Lipp. When the general manager said, "Herr Greb, I would like you to meet Herr Lipp," Greb burst into laughter. Some time later, after the two men became good friends, Lipp asked Greb why he had laughed during their initial meeting. Greb tried to explain, but later confessed that he was never really certain that Herr Lipp fully understood.

✝

Another story from Larry involved a meeting of Japanese marketing executives in Tokyo. The secretary to the general manager, Miss Ito, read aloud the names of those present to assure them that their airline reservations were safely in hand. She easily pronounced the names of the Japanese executives present: "Mr. Hiedo Miayke, Mr. Naushiee Konishi, Mr. Norio Morisuti, Mr. Tadashi Mikorira, Mr. Tomoko Takahashi . . . ," and so on. But when she got to "Larry Greb" she halted, stuttered, tried over and over again, and finally succeeded. Later, Greb asked if there had been any problem with his air ticket. Miss Ito apologized and politely explained: "Oh, so sorry. No problem there. It is just that the name 'Larry Greb' is a very, very difficult name for a Japanese person to pronounce." Where Greb would trip and stumble over the pronunciation of the complex Japanese names, his short, three-syllable name proved almost impossible to say by the Japanese.

Larry later noted that in written correspondence with his Japanese counterparts, his name would often appear as "Mr. Rarry Gleb." Also, instead of referring to one Johnson brand name as "Klear Floor Wax," for the Japanese it would come out as "Queer for Wax."

✝

Several years ago, Greb received a phone call from one of Johnson Wax's senior purchasing managers who asked if Larry could help locate the country of Taiwan on a map he had on the desk in front of him. Greb told him to first locate Japan on the map; the man at the other end of the phone did so with no problem. Then Greb then asked him if he could find Hong

Kong, which he also did. Greb then told him to move right, or east of Hong Kong, and south and left of Japan. There was silence until the manager asked, "Is it anywhere near Formosa?" Greb replied, "Yes. That's it. Taiwan *is* Formosa. That name change occurred almost fifty years ago . . . and you need a new map!"

+

In Larry's early days with Johnson Wax, he was responsible for the sales and distribution of the company's products to the overseas military and other government agencies. It was early in his career, and he recalls that he and his colleagues were inclined to stage practical jokes on one another. For example, one would call the other and identify himself as Mr. I. P. Daly, author of the famous book *Yellow River*. About this time, Greb received a call from a person who identified herself as Francoise Schwartz. Greb immediately thought it was a joke, and so he quickly replied, "Oh, sure. I know your brother, Bermuda Schwartz." The voice at the other end responded with an indignant "Pardon me?" It turned out that the caller was indeed Francoise Schwartz, head of an important company by the same name that supplied U.S.-made products to all the U.S. embassies around the world. In other words, the caller was potentially an extremely important customer. Greb apologized profusely. In later years, Greb met Schwartz personally, explained about the practical jokes, and they became good friends.

Funny Travel Trick Number Two

When you travel in certain parts of the world, it is common to spot other American businesspeople who seem to be on the same travel schedule as you. In South America, for example, a businessperson might spend three days in São Paulo, then three days in Buenos Aires, three days in Santiago, and so on.

In those cases, it is common to see the same American again and again in the airport and on your flight.

On one of these occasions I observed one particular man who would always sit at a window seat . . . *and then keep the two seats next to him completely unoccupied.* I, meanwhile, would always seem to be assigned to that crowded middle seat—often with the person next to me carrying a chicken or some smelly package in his lap—and watch enviously as my compatriot spread his work out and prepared for the next city. Finally, in the airport in Lima, I approached him, saying, "Pardon me, we've shared several flights now, and I'm very curious about something. I note that you always get a window seat and somehow manage to keep the two seats next to you unoccupied. How do you do that? Do you buy those seats, or what?"

"Oh, no," he replied. "I couldn't afford that. But I do have a special trick that always seems to work. If you like, I'll teach it to you."

Assuring him that I did, I watched as he reached into his travel briefcase and produced a baby's pacifier. He said, "Among other things, my company makes these. So I always carry samples with me. Then, whenever I make reservations on an airplane, I request a window seat. As people board the airplane, if it appears they are going to sit down in the seats next to me, I merely take out one of these samples . . . put it in my mouth . . . and look up at them." He then demonstrated.

After a brief pause, he added, "Now, tell me the truth. Would *you* sit down next to a grown man sucking on a pacifier??"

Clearing Customs in Style

A friend of mine in the pen business traveled to Brazil periodically to visit his company's factory there. In the manufacturing of a fountain pen, one of the most essential parts is the tiny metal pellet at the end of the nib—literally, the point of the pen. This part is critical because, quite obviously, it is the part that meets the paper when writing. That pellet must be exceedingly durable and is therefore usually made from several

*"I merely take out one of these . . . put it in my mouth . . .
and look up at them."*

exotic metals. Consequently, it is quite costly. As it happened, the country of Brazil was very restrictive about the importation of these particular pellets and required extensive paperwork and heavy duties. Since several thousand of the pellets—each about the size of a pinhead—could be carried in a container the size of a common medicine bottle, it was always tempting for the pen executives to carry them into the country without declaring them at customs. My friend decided to do exactly that, taking the chance that the customs official would not notice one innocent-looking prescription bottle. As it happened, my friend chanced to encounter an eagle-eye customs agent who, while examining his luggage, picked up the bottle of pellets, shook it, and said, "What are these?" Without hesitation, my friend answered, "Oh, those are my iron pills." The agent shook the bottle again and was just about to ask another question when my quick-thinking friend said, "By the way . . . what time is it?" Looking at his watch, the official said, "Three o'clock." "Oops," said my friend. "It's time to take one of my pills." Prying off the cap, he carefully spilled some of the pellets into the palm of his hand, took one in his fingers, popped it into his mouth, and swallowed. Satisfied, the customs agent said, "OK. Go on through."

+

A friend of mine happened to be doing business in Bogotá, Colombia, near the date of his twenty-fifth wedding anniversary. Aware that Colombia was the world-famous source for the world's highest quality emeralds, he decided that this would be a perfect opportunity to buy his wife an emerald ring as an anniversary present. Throughout Latin America, only naive shoppers walk into retail stores and buy articles without haggling or having some type of special connection, especially when it comes to expensive jewelry. Consequently, when the American explained his intention to his business representative in Bogotá, the latter assured him he personally knew a reputable jeweler who would assuredly offer a quality emerald at the lowest possible price. In the store, and after examining several dozen rings, the American selected one and asked the price. The jeweler tapped some figures into his calculator, converted them into U.S. dollars and said, "Well, the normal retail price would be eighteen hundred dollars, but, of course, since you are an associate of my good friend here, I can let you have it for only nine hundred." The man's local associate assured him that would be a satisfactory price, so the deal was sealed. The jeweler then said, "Of course, you don't want to pay duty on the ring, so I'll give you a receipt for only three hundred dollars (which, at that time, was the allowable maximum for Americans to spend and be able to bring their purchases back into the United States without paying duties)." The American businessman protested, saying, "No, I don't want to get into trouble with U.S. customs. If I do, and my name is placed on the 'watch' list, I'll have trouble every time I pass in and out of the States." Both Colombians scoffed at that objection, saying it was silly and unnecessary to pay extra duties.

They insisted it would be perfectly safe for the American to bring the ring back to the United States with a receipt showing the cost was only $300. The American finally relented. However, during the flight home he became more and more uneasy. He thought: "What if they recognize the true value? Those customs officials must be trained to judge the value of jewelry, especially emeralds on flights coming from Colombia." By the time my friend landed at the Miami airport, he was perspiring and lamenting to himself, "I bet I fit the perfect profile of a smuggler!"

Finally, as his turn arrived at the customs desk, the officer asked the usual question: "Anything to declare?" In response, my friend guiltily handed him the box containing the ring. "Do you have a receipt for this?" the agent asked. My friend produced the false receipt and the agent looked first at the receipt, then at the ring, then back at the receipt. Shaking his head back and forth, the agent finally said, "Boy . . . they sure get a lot of money for these rings, don't they?" Stunned, my friend very nearly blurted out: "Wait a moment! Three hundred dollars? Do you want to know how much I *really* paid for that ring?"

Fortunately, he said nothing. The agent motioned him on, and he left the airport wondering if . . . just maybe . . . the ring actually was *not worth even $300!*

⊥

Businesspeople who travel from Colombia to Mexico become accustomed to long delays recovering their luggage. One reason is that because of the drug trade this connection has become a popular traffic route. On one of these occasions, I remember standing in the baggage area of the Mexico City airport late one night watching as porters took all the luggage from our incoming flight and spread it along a single line. Then, a customs officer with a dog trained to sniff drugs started at the end of the line and carefully paused before each piece of luggage. One American businessman standing next to me said, "Boy, I just bought that luggage. It's genuine leather. I hope the cow that leather came from wasn't in heat when it died." An American on the other side of me responded, "Yeah, that's a worry. In my case I've got some dirty laundry in there that hasn't been touched in weeks. It's liable to blow the nose right off that dog."

Unintentionally Humorous Travels in England

An elderly American woman was visiting England as part of a tour group, guided by a friendly local driver. They drove into a small village north of the town of Windsor and near Heathrow Airport and came upon a lovely old English church. The woman asked the tour guide when the church had been built. "About six hundred and fifty years ago," he explained. "It's a pity," the woman said, "they built it so close to the airport." The polite driver/guide agreed without further comment.

✝

When my family and I moved to England for a four-year business assignment, we would often spend weekends touring some of the famous British castles and churches. On one of those occasions, we visited Windsor Castle, home of British royalty. In the large chapel there, visitors pass numerous tombs holding past royals surrounded by religious sculptures and inscriptions. In the hush of the moment, our five-year-old son suddenly looked up at his mother and blurted out, "There! Now, there, mother! Now there! *Now* don't you believe in God??"

On another of these excursions, we attended a service in a beautiful old English countryside church. My wife tried to keep our seven-year-old daughter occupied with crayons and a coloring book, but she was obviously becoming impatient over the lengthy service. Finally, she whispered a question to her mother: "Why do those windows have those colored pictures?" My wife explained that they were called stained glass windows and that they were memorials to people who had died in the service. My daughter then asked, "Would that have been at the seven o'clock service or the nine-thirty service?"

✝

During my work assignment in England, I became a bona fide commuter, spending up to two hours each day riding trains from my home in the county of Sussex to London and back. From my clothing and general appearance, I was easily spotted as an American. While the British are world-renowned for respecting other people's privacy, on numerous occasions during that long span of time some of my fellow commuters would uncharacteristically strike up a conversation. This was especially true if and when they heard my distinct American accent. I realized they were trying to be friendly and hospitable to a visitor, but it eventually became something of a nuisance. The conversation and questions followed a definite pattern: "How do you like our weather?" "Where are you from in America?" And so on. Because the vastness of the United States was so unappreciated, one particularly nettling question was, "Oh, I have a cousin in the city of Toledo (or Kansas City, or Portland, or wherever). Now, is there any chance that you would know him?"

After repeated incidents like this, I must confess I started to avoid such interactions, preferring to bury myself in my newspaper. I actually developed an early warning system that alerted me to these incoming salvos: I would watch their eyes; after a time, one could sense that the person was becoming more and more curious, and, soon, the predictable line of questioning would begin. On one of these occasions, while glancing over the top of my newspaper, I started receiving the now-familiar signals from a mustached fellow in heavy tweeds sitting across from me: an attempt at eye contact, a raising of the eyebrows, a slight opening of the lips. But on this particular day, I was feeling especially unfriendly, so I simply raised the newspaper and blotted out his gaze. Each time my newspaper fell lower, I could see the overture starting anew. Fortunately, I was able to block his attempts for the duration of the trip, and when we reached Victoria Station I quickly disembarked. Walking along on the station platform, I could sense the man closely behind me, and I heard his footsteps coming closer and closer. Finally, I felt a gentle tap on my shoulder and heard the ubiquitous English phrase "Pahdon me." I knew I had been trapped by this persistent fellow. As I prepared to endure his familiar words, he looked down his nose, pointed to my trousers, and simply said, "Pahdon me . . . but your zippah is open." And he turned and walked away.

Never again did I reject a moment of friendly eye contact.

☦

The matter of respecting another person's privacy, as just related, is no casual societal trait in England. The older generation, especially, tends to adhere to this rule. For example, in the United States the most common conversational gambit at an American cocktail gathering is to ask, "What do you do?" meaning, of course, "What do you do for a living?" But in English society, this could be—and often is—considered an invasion of privacy. I learned of this particular taboo after only a short time of living and working in England. In fact, it then became something of a personal challenge to meet new and different people and see how long I could refrain from falling back on that familiar and—to me—innocent question.

At one point in our stay, we moved to a new furnished residence in the picturesque town of Reigate, in the county of Surrey, about twenty-five miles south of London. Within a short time, acquaintances there arranged for us to be invited to a rather large cocktail party where, naturally, my wife and I were introduced to many new faces. I relished this opportunity to practice my newly acquired skill at avoiding, at all costs, that forbidden question, "What do you do?"

As the party warmed, I was introduced to a distinguished

gentleman and we quickly proceeded through the rote of talking about the weather, central heating, animals, and children—all standard and safe areas of inquiry. But during our conversation I detected a growing curiosity in him. I could sense he was becoming more and more anxious to learn exactly why I was living in England. Finally, he asked somewhat sheepishly, "What brings you to our country?" I thought, "Aha! First point for me!" I looked at him confidently and, with a smile, answered, "My firm sent me here." He muttered a few more words, but I could see the central question was still eating away. He continued: "Oh. And what type of business is your firm in?" Game point for me! But I silently noted that he still had not asked the climactic question: What is the *name* of your firm? Again, I offered him an enigmatic smile and simply replied, "Oh, we are in the writing instrument business." Finally, with a sigh of resignation but overcome by curiosity, he said, "And may I ask what is the name of your firm?" Set and match to me! I had won the game. When I, figuratively speaking, offered my hand to the loser over the net, I responded, "The Parker Pen Company." "Good God!" he burst out. "We are your agents in Nigeria. My colleagues mentioned to me that some young businessperson from Parker had been transferred from America to London and might be taking up residence south of London, but I did not know you would be living here in Reigate."

Somewhat disappointed, I concluded, "A hollow victory." He was playing the game with a different incentive and motive from my own.

As a moral to this short story, try this test of your conversational skills. At any large social gathering here in the United States, or especially in England, when you are meeting new people, try to refrain from asking the core question, "What do you do?" See how long you can survive. If your conversation mate asks that question first, consider yourself as having acquired a minor victory. Add points to your score if you can respond with obscure answers. The longer you can survive, the more mysterious you become.

How and When to Use Humor

Americans seem to have a worldwide reputation for being friendly, informal, monolingual, and at times, a trifle loud. Psychologists tell us this is the result of certain strains of insecurity and apprehension. We are uncomfortable crossing major cultural bridges because we don't get much practice dealing with significantly different cultures. In Europe, travel 500 miles in any direction, and you'll cross four, five, or more different cultural enclaves. For most Americans, we must travel thousands of miles to find just one (Mexico or French Canada). As a result, when we do travel abroad, we want to make instant friends. One way to do that is to be humorous. I believe each of us deep down wants to make people smile, laugh, and enjoy us. Unfortunately, that leads me back to "a trifle loud." I cannot count the number of times I have been in some remote hotel overseas and been embarrassed by hearing a group of loud Americans—often making light of some local scene, food, person, or situation. *Moral: Humor is a delightful way to ingratiate yourself, but so is listening and learning. Pack those qualities in your suitcase when you travel abroad.*

More Advice

Here are ten general tips for more successful travel:

1. Leave copies of your itinerary with friends, neighbors, and business associates back home. Also, put a copy in your suitcase—in the event your bag is lost, that itinerary will help officials track you down.
2. Make a photocopy of your passport and put that in your suitcase, too. An old, expired passport works just as well. If you should lose your passport while traveling, or if it is stolen, when you have proof that you already have one it is much easier to have a new passport issued at the nearest U.S. Embassy or Consulate.

3. Always carry a "survival kit" with you—a small carry-on bag filled with essentials: toiletries, medicines, glasses, reading material, pen, jewelry and other valuables, passport, air tickets, motion-sickness and pain medicine, and sleeping aids. To be *really* prepared, add these items: change of underwear, sunscreen, eye mask, earplugs, neck pillow, and perhaps even a full change of clothes. With these "survival" items, you can withstand the loss of your luggage for a surprisingly long time.

4. As for money matters, try to travel with at least two popular credit cards for charging purchases and for use at ATMs (automated teller machines). More and more travelers are reporting that they receive good currency exchange rates when withdrawing local currencies using their ATM cards. Carrying several hundred dollars in U.S. traveler's checks is also a good precaution (in the event your cards aren't accepted). Avoid carrying large amounts of cash.

5. Whenever you check into a hotel, and if you are unacquainted with tipping practices, ask the concierge for some advice. Many hotels, especially in Europe, automatically add a service charge to hotel and restaurant bills.

6. Visit a travel specialty store before you go. More and more are available. Rand McNally, for example, has several dozen such stores scattered across the United States. Another good, reliable source is your local library. A few hours of reading about your destination will add immeasurably to your trip.

7. One handy but little known aid is a small booklet printed by the U.S. Government titled *Key Officers of Foreign Service Posts*. This publication provides the addresses and telephone numbers, plus personnel listing, for all U.S. embassies, missions, and consulates around the world. To obtain a copy contact the U.S. Government Printing Office, P.O. Box 37194, Pittsburgh, PA 15250, (202) 783-3238.

8. Check with your insurance agent to review your cover-

age while traveling outside the country. Remember, too, that Medicare benefits apply only while you are in North America, and other medical plans cover only emergency care while overseas. Supplemental policies of all kinds are available through your local agent.

9. Packing for a long trip can be a real challenge. One maxim among experienced travelers is, "Pack half as much as you think you need, and take twice as much money." As for packing clothes, the best single piece of advice I was ever given was to pack any item that might wrinkle in individual plastic bags—the kind you get from the dry cleaner's.

10. Keep a journal. It can occupy those inevitable occasions of inactivity such as waiting for trains, buses, cars, airplanes, or friends. It is all too easy to forget some of the things you enjoyed while traveling, and a few notes or reminders will jog your brain and bring back a flood of memories.

12

Misunderstandings

When the American baseball player Bill Gullickson signed a phenomenal contract to play baseball in Japan, he was asked what daily life was like in Japan. He replied that the language was the most difficult and different feature. "It's crazy," he said. "The only American words I saw were Sony and Mitsubishi."

There are several obvious reasons why we misunderstand one another in our daily communication. Consider the following:

- We speak at a rate of about 100 to 110 words per minute.
- We can actually hear at a rate of about 400 words a minute. In other words, we could record a person's voice, play his or her speech back at a very high speed, and still comprehend what was said.
- The most significant factor is that we can *think* at a rate of about 800 words a minute.

That means that we are listening only about 15 to 20 percent of the time, because our minds are capable of racing around and about, thinking about other things, and still piecing together what is being said at the snail-paced 110 words a minute. Consequently, many of us have not acquired good listening skills.

Scientists suggest that fully 60 percent of all misunderstandings are due to poor listening habits.

Add to this mix the fact that there are about 750,000 words in the English language. Ours is an opulent language, and, as we learned earlier in this book, we throw in idioms, slang, jargon, metaphors, buzzwords, acronyms, and sports and military terminology, which make our language a moving target for anyone who has not learned it thoroughly.

As this book testifies, misunderstandings are particularly common when traveling overseas or when hosting international visitors. But to demonstrate that they can occur just as easily in our own language, and in our own culture, consider this story: Bob Collins is a well-known figure in my small town—a prominent attorney, president of the local school board, chairman of Little League baseball, member of the Police and Fire Commission, and so on. His wife, Trish, and their young son, Daniel, were at the local shopping mall when a friend approached and said, "Why, hello, Trish. How are you?" Then, turning to young Dan, he asked, "And who are you, young man?" Dan dutifully replied "I'm Bob Collins's son." "Oh, of course," the man said. "Everyone knows Bob."

Later that day, Trish took Daniel aside and explained, "That was nice that you would identify yourself as Bob Collins's son, but you must remember that you are an individual—you are your own person, your own personality, you have your own identity. Remember that next time."

A week later, when Trish and Daniel were walking down the street, a similar incident occurred. A friend approached Trish, said hello, and then turned to Dan and said, "And you must be Bob Collins's son." Whereupon Dan looked him squarely in the eye and said, "No, sir. No, I'm not. My mother told me I'm not."

Clearly Funny Communication

The opposite of misunderstandings is, of course, clear communication. For example, one of my favorite aphorisms is: "Good writing is clear thinking made visible." An example of clear communication is found in the following short but expressive letter of thanks written by a young girl named Amber after her third-grade class visited a nearby farm. She wrote:

> Dear Mr. Farmer,
>
> Thank you for letting us visit your farm. Also, thank you for letting the rabbit poop on Tony.
>
> Signed,
Amber

✝

From our nation's history, we have a wonderful example of clear communication in a single piece of correspondence. It was written on March 16, 1813, by the commander of His Britannic Majesty's Ship Portiers, anchored in the mouth of Delaware Bay:

> Sir,
>
> As soon as you receive this, I request you will send twenty live bullock with a proportionate quantity of vegetables, and hay to the Portiers for the use of Britanic [sic] Majesty's Squadron now at this anchorage which shall be immediately paid for at the Philadelphia prices; if you refuse to comply with this request I shall be under necessity of destroying your town.
>
> I have the honor to be, Sir, Your
Very obedient Servant
J. P. Beresford, Commodore
& Commander of this British
Squadron in the Mouth of
The Delaware

Americans Say the Darnedest Things

To demonstrate once again that misunderstandings happen in our own culture, and in our own language, every day and in every situation, here are some examples I have collected over the years.

✝

A great source for misstatements is the job application form. People make mistakes without realizing it. There is always a section called "Describe last job duties." Here is what some people actually replied:

- One person meant to say he was a "sales clerk." Instead he wrote he had been a "sales cluck."
- Another had been a carpenter. He wrote he was a "crapender."
- A third had been a forklift operator in a warehouse; he wrote he "Ran a frocklift in the whorehouse."

Another section of the job application form asks for the "Reason for leaving last job." One person wrote "fried" instead of "fired." A woman obviously could have said "maternity" but instead wrote, "laid due to pregnancy."

✝

Labor negotiations at the bargaining table produce some wonderful examples of misstatements and misunderstandings. Negotiators on both sides tend to get heated and emotional. The result is statements like these:

- "Ah, well, now the penguin has swung the other way."
- "We are adamant. We just want to be flexible."
- "These men can hear what you're saying; they're not blind."

✝

Visit your state capitol and listen to some of the statements— or misstatements—made by your elected representatives on the legislative floors. Here are some actual excerpts from legislative minutes:

- "Wait a moment—I misquoted myself."
- "This body is becoming entirely too laxative about some matters."
- "I smell a rat and intend to nip it in the bud."
- "I think I know more about this bill than I understand."
- "There comes a time to put principles aside and do what's right."
- "It's time to grab the bull by the tail and look it squarely in the eye."
- "People planning on getting in serious accidents should wear seatbelts."
- "This is a good health bill. Take it from one who has survived a terminal heart attack."
- "As long as I am a senator, there won't be any nuclear suppositories in my district!"

✝

We contribute to misunderstandings and misstatements in innocent ways. Take, for example, when harried parents write notes to teachers explaining why their children missed a day of school. Here are excerpts from some actual notes:

- "Please eckuse [sic] John been absent on January 28, 29, 30, 31, 32, and 33."
- "My son is under the doctor's care and should not take P.E. Please execute him."
- "Please excuse Joe Friday. He had loose vowels."
- "Carlos was absent from school yesterday. Because he was playing football. He was hurt in the growing part."
- "Please excuse Johnny from being. It was his father's fault."
- "Mary Ann was absent November 11 because she had a fever, sore throat, headache, and upset stomach, her sister was also sick—fever, sore throat. Her brother had a low-

grade temp. And a gall all over. I wasn't feeling the best either, sore throat, fever. There must be the flu going around. Even her father got hot last night."

✝

Courtroom bloopers abound. Mary Louise Gilman, editor of the *National Shorthand Reporter,* has collected dozens of them in her two books, *Humor in the Court* (1977) and *More Humor in the Court* (1994). Here are just three examples of "transquips" between attorneys and witnesses:

Q. Doctor, did you say he was shot in the woods?
A. No. I said he was shot in the lumbar region.

Q. Do you know how far pregnant you are right now?
A. I will be three months on November eighth.
Q. Apparently then, the date of conception was August eighth?
A. Yes.
Q. What were you and your husband doing at that time?

Q. (Questioning a teenager) And lastly, Gary, all your responses must be oral. OK? What school do you go to?
A. Oral.
Q. How old are you?
A. Oral.

✝

Marshall Johnston is a retired newspaper executive who collects newspaper headlines from around the world that contain double entendres. Here are a few from his collection:

From the *International Herald Tribune:*
POLICE DISCOVER CRACK IN AUSTRALIA

From the *Edmonton* (Alberta, Canada) *Journal:*
SEXUAL MISCONDUCT ALLEGED AT CITY HALL

From the *Denver Post:*
FRENCH OFFER TERRORIST REWARD

From the *Philadelphia Inquirer:*
N.J. JUDGE TO RULE ON NUDE BEACH

When Yogi Berra was told that the new mayor of Dublin, Ireland, was Jewish . . . and a woman! . . . his response was, "Only in America."

Carrying Our Misunderstandings Abroad—with Humor

When my family and I lived in England, we were walking down the "high street" (main street) of our village one day when we were attracted to a large, upright public scale. At that time, the British measured human weight in terms of "stones," with one stone equal to fourteen pounds. I mentally calculated that since I weighed 184 pounds, the scale should indicate I weighed "13 stone, 2 pounds." Anxious to enlighten my wife on this British peculiarity, I stepped on the scale, inserted a coin, and watched as a printed card emerged. On one side of the card was my fortune, which I read aloud to my wife: "You are charming, witty, and attractive to other people. Your intelligence is immediately obvious and people often turn to you for advice on how to do things." Handing the card to my wife, she read the fortune, turned the card over, read the words "13 stone, 2 pounds," and said: "They've got your weight wrong, too."

Postscript: Since that time, the English have switched to the metric system, where 2.2 pounds equals 1 kilogram. So the same confusion could continue—my 185 pounds now translates to 84 kilos.

☩

Ron Alexander compiles a regular column for the *New York Times* called "Metropolitan Diary," which consists of stories contributed by readers. Here are two of them involving Americans visiting London:

> Marks & Spencer is a famous chain of clothing stores in England. When Milton Prigoff was in London he overheard two American women discussing their shopping experiences. One of them said: "I was in Marks & Spencer with several dresses over my arm, looking for a fitting room. After a while, I located an employee wearing a badge and asked for the location of the fitting rooms. 'I'm sorry I can't help you,' she said. 'I'm in customer relations.'"

> Phyllis Weiss was walking downstairs to a ladies room in a Soho restaurant, thinking about the sometimes puzzling symbols used to mark the doors. Luckily, though, the restrooms in that restaurant were merely labeled "M" and "W." Since they were both closed, she waited. The "M" door opened and a man walked out. Moments later, the "W" door opened and a different man walked out. With some shock she said, "I didn't expect to see a man walk out of a door with a 'W' on it." The man looked at her, looked at the sign on the door, paused, and simply said: "Whomever."

☦

Richard R. Gesteland is a twenty-six-year veteran businessman who has lived at various times in six major cities around the world. He now resides in Madison, Wisconsin, and is a consultant on how to negotiate among different cultures, with major corporate clients both in the United States and around the world. Here he recounts two stories from his past involving misunderstandings:

> Driving across France on the way to our first overseas assignment, my wife, Hopi, and I stopped at a small country hotel in Normandy. Since the night clerk spoke no English I decided to impress Hopi with my command of the local lingo.
>
> All went well at check-in until the clerk said we would have to move our car to a new spot before 7 A.M. the next

morning. When I asked him in my best French to give us an early wake-up call so I could move the car, he and all the people within earshot suddenly burst out in uproarious laughter. I recall one old guy laughing so hard his false teeth popped out.

In our room a few minutes later, Hopi gently explained that what I had said in French was, "Please wake me up early yesterday so I can carry the car off the market square."

It took me twenty years to get even. The occasion arose while I was touring a French-owned Moroccan leather goods factory with my company's buyer of handbags. Struck by the quality and style of the production, I asked the attractive Frenchwoman in charge of exports, "Do you exhibit your handbags at major fashion shows?" Translating directly from French, the young woman replied, "But of course! Why, this year for example, we exposed ourselves all over Europe."

I wonder how the French say, "He who laughs last, laughs best"?

✝

Learning to understand a new culture is always a challenging experience. Robert Ma, who managed a franchise in China for a major American fast-food chain, provided these twelve "golden rules" for living, working, and understanding that country.

1. Everything is possible.
2. Nothing is easy.
3. Western business logic does not apply.
4. It is a fun project if there is no deadline.
5. You must persist—things will come your way eventually.
6. Patience is the essence of success.
7. "You don't know China" means they disagree.
8. "New regulation" means they found a new way to avoid doing something.
9. "Internal regulation" means they are mad at you.

10. "Basically, no problem" means *big* problem.
11. When you are optimistic, think about Rule #2.
12. When you are discouraged, think about Rule #1.

✝

During the first winter of our assignment in England, the antiquated central heating system in our rented home sputtered and stopped. I was told it would take one week to obtain spare parts. Thus, my wife, three young children, and I faced the depressing prospect of seven days of damp, bone-chilling British weather. To add to our plight, my wife was facing extensive dental surgery. A kindly neighbor, hearing of our situation, offered to loan us a paraffin burner. In my mind, as an American, paraffin means the waxy substance used in making candles. But, desperate as I was, I decided even the meager heat afforded by a few candles would be better than nothing. So I hurried to buy some paraffin at the "ironmonger" store, complimenting myself for knowing that's what they called a hardware store in England. "Oh, we don't carry paraffin here, sir," was the reply. "You purchase that at the petrol station across the street." Once again, translating that into American, I headed for the nearby gas station. "Yes, we carry paraffin," the attendant confirmed. "But where is your tin?" he asked. I looked at him dumbly. "Tin?" I asked, imagining myself stuffing wax into a tin. "Yes, sir. You'll need a tin. You can purchase one at the ironmongers." Reversing my tracks, I purchased my tin and presented it to the attendant at the petrol station. He then walked to a large metal drum and began pouring kerosene into my tin. It finally dawned on me that in England, "paraffin" was the word for kerosene. Survival in England, I discovered, was going to mean an everyday conflict with misunderstandings.

✝

Our second daughter, Kathi, was eight years old when we returned to the United States after four years in England. Con-

The author being warmed by British paraffin burners.

sequently, her knowledge of American geography and American traditions was minimal. We enrolled her in an elementary school and watched and listened carefully when she returned home each day to detect if she was having any particular problems adjusting to her new American education. First, we noticed she had difficulty remembering if Philadelphia was a city or a state. Second, we knew she was embarrassed whenever the teacher asked her to recite in class because of her delightful acquired English accent. And so it went. One evening she returned home and when I asked what she had learned that day she replied, "Oh, we learned some delightful new American songs. One was called 'Gawd Bless America,' and the otha' was a peculiah one called 'The Star Bannered Spaniel.'"

How and When to Use Humor

At this point, it might be useful to review some general suggestions for how and when to use humor:

- Bear in mind that American humor is difficult to export because we rely so heavily on topical humor, current events, and wordplay. Each of these requires an intimate knowledge of the American scene and the American dialect.
- Avoid all ethnic-type jokes and anything that might be considered as smutty, off-color, scatological, rude, embarrassing, or downright obscene.
- Never, of course, make jokes about religions.
- Try to note what type of humor appeals to those around you. You can then test the waters of humor, but do it slowly and cautiously. Also, discuss this universal conundrum with your associates overseas: Each culture has its own distinctive sense of humor, and each of us wishes to share humorous stories and incidents. So how can we do that safely? That is the question to present to your confreres.
- If in doubt, don't. In other words, if you have any sense of doubt about the appropriateness of, let's say, a witty remark resting on the tip of your tongue, swallow it. When telling jokes in an overseas setting, four things can happen, only one of them good. Those four things are: (1) your story is understood and appreciated; (2) your story is taken as rude and improper; (3) your story is considered as sarcasm and is unappreciated; and (4) the most likely scenario, your story is incomprehensible to your audience.
- Finally, as we advised back in Chapter 5, if and when you commit some goof or gaffe, try to "laugh it off." This action demonstrates that you can laugh at yourself, an admired quality in almost any culture.

More Advice

Here are some factors to consider when walking through the maze of different cultures around the world:

1. Misunderstandings often arise from what is *not* said, or what is "written between the lines." Edward T. Hall, the

famed social anthropologist, explains that societies with "high context" communication, such as the Japanese, rely strongly on intuition when communicating. In fact, much of their communication is unspoken; it is implied or understood without verbalizing. Americans, on the other hand, dislike this subtlety; we are considered "low context" communicators because we like everything spelled out in detail with lots of words. As examples, Hall points to twin brothers or sisters. Such siblings have high-context communication abilities: they understand each other easily, quickly, and without verbalizing. At the opposite end, two American lawyers rely less and less on context and prefer to specify every point and every thought using an abundance of words. The best example of this divergence between Japanese and American communications involves the word "yes." In ordinary conversations, the Japanese will often nod their heads and say "yes." Americans believe they are saying, "Yes, I agree." However, in the Japanese culture it is impolite to introduce negatives, or to disrupt the harmony of a situation; therefore, it is both impolite and improper to say "no." Consequently, when they say "yes" they are really saying, "Yes, I hear you—but that doesn't necessarily mean I agree with you." Similarly, among high-context cultures like the Japanese, a reply such as, "Oh, that might be very difficult" carries the very clear implication, "No, that is not possible."

2. Watch the eyes. In fact, as we pointed out in Chapter 6, Gestures, watch for all types of body language. But the eyes are especially important. Among some cultures, it is believed that the eyes are the windows of the soul. And when trying to communicate with other cultures, you'll find a person's eyes will tell you much about comprehension. The exception is among Asian cultures, where direct eye contact is considered impolite. But if in your conversations, the other person's mind seems to disappear from behind his or her eyes, it's time to stop, retreat, and retrace your verbal steps to try to regain attention.

3. Be careful with numbers. Write them down or repeat them. In some languages (such as Japanese), numbers are

stated in forms that are different from our system. For example, in Japanese one million is expressed as "one-hundred, ten-thousands."

4. When traveling overseas, never assume that people around you do not understand English. For instance, when in a public setting such as public transportation, it's tempting to assume that because you do not hear any English your fellow passengers do not comprehend it. Americans are sometimes guilty of making critical remarks about the living conditions, the conveyance, or even about the local people when it's entirely possible that a local person within earshot understands English.

5. Use visual aids wherever possible. For example, if you are unable to get someone to understand a key word, point to it in a bilingual dictionary. If you are asking directions, use a map to trace the route rather than relying on verbal instructions. Play charades—if that will help you make a point or explain your question.

6. Alcohol may reduce your inhibitions and tempt you into thinking you can communicate or speak the local language more easily, but usually anything that dulls our senses or our awareness is counterproductive to comprehension. A glass of wine may help you relax and improve your wit and expression, but a whole bottle will not necessarily turn you into an international raconteur.

7. Finally, summarize, paraphrase, and echo. Repeat (in different forms) what you are saying and hearing. One diplomatic device is to say, "I know that sometimes I speak very fast. Perhaps it would be helpful to stop and review. Perhaps you can relate back to me, in your own words, what we have discussed."

Finally, review the advice provided at the end of Chapter 1, Words.

13

Miscellaneous Humor

I once gave one of my books to my boss. He seemed very pleased, and he fussed and complimented me over the book. He asked me to be sure to sign it and declared he would be anxious to read it. Two years later, I returned to his home and—sure enough—there on his living room coffee table was the very same book. I picked it up, examined it . . . and found a bookmark on page seven!

There are bright spots as an author, however. One fringe benefit is that on certain occasions, one of the network TV talk shows may invite you for an interview. ABC's *Good Morning America* has been particularly kind to me. Three guest shots were prompted by new books, and two more appearances resulted from national news events. One of the latter occasions was in 1991 during the Gulf War with Iraq. The producers wanted insights on what cultural differences our military personnel might encounter in Saudi Arabia. Accordingly, they sent me an air ticket and booked a room for me at the hotel that customarily hosted the show's guests.

When I arrived at the hotel reception desk, I gave my name to the two young women there and explained that I had a reservation. Entering my name into her computer, the first young woman read the screen and said, "Oh! You're booked in the *Good Morning America* suite." I responded, "That's nice." She continued: "And there's a message that Harold, your limousine driver, will be here tomorrow morning at 6:45 A.M. to pick you up. Also, you are supposed to just sign for any charges you have tonight." She gave me my key, I thanked her, turned around, and headed toward the elevator. As I was walking away, I overheard the second clerk ask in a whispered voice, "Who was that??" The first one replied, "Oh . . . that was nobody."

Obviously they are more accustomed to greeting Robert Redford or Elton John than some unknown writer from Wisconsin.

Still, the next morning the interview seemed to go well, and, despite being a "nobody," I went back to Chicago where I then transferred to a flight for Phoenix. Sitting on the plane next to me were two elderly women. As we engaged in conversation, I learned they were retired schoolteachers heading for a vacation in sunny Arizona. I happened to have some page proofs from a new book I was writing and began paging through them. The nearest woman became curious and this dialogue ensued:

WOMAN: Oh, is that a manuscript for a book?
ME: Yes.
WOMAN: Are you an author?
ME: Yes.
WOMAN: Is that your newest book?
ME: Yes.
WOMAN: Have you written other books?
ME: Well . . . yes.
WOMAN: Oh, have you ever appeared on television?
ME: Well . . . as a matter of fact, yes.
WOMAN (More and more curious): What shows?
ME: Well, have you ever happened to watch *Good Morning America*?
WOMAN (Excited): Oh, yes! (Nudging her partner) We watch it every morning.

"Oh . . . that was nobody."

ME: Did you happen to watch it yesterday morning?

WOMAN (Excited): Yes! Yes, we did!

ME: Well . . . I was on yesterday.

WOMAN (Turning to her companion, she carried on a rather long whispered conversation. Finally, she turned back to me and said rather severely): We didn't see you!

Then she turned away very coolly and didn't talk with me the rest of the trip. I could just imagine her arriving in Phoenix and warning her friends to "be very, very careful whom you converse with on airplanes. The man who sat next to us claimed he had appeared on *Good Morning America* the day before. We saw that program! We didn't see him! The nerve of some people."

The Book Tour: Ten Humorous Discoveries

One of the unique experiences for an author is an event called a "book tour." Your publisher sends you off for several weeks at a time, usually visiting a new city every day, to promote your book. Each morning an escort picks you up and drives you from radio station to radio station for interviews on daily talk shows. Then perhaps you are taken to a midday TV show, then the local newspaper to meet the book reviewer, perhaps a couple more radio stations, and then to a late-afternoon conversation with a magazine writer. It can be a grueling marathon, but it can also be gratifying—after all, how else could you talk about yourself and your writing over and over again? Still, the crowded airports, the airplanes packed with people, the poor food, the delays, and the poor weather—all those tend to sour such a tour. As I embarked on one of these book tours, I complained to my wife, "I don't know why I let myself in for these things." She thought for a moment and then replied, "Do you suppose you do it for the attention?" Point made.

The publicity tours are educational, however. Following is a list of ten discoveries from one of them:

1. Following one tour, twenty-three people wrote me to say they knew *other* people named Axtell and wanted to know if I was related. In every case I was not.
2. One woman wrote saying she saw me on TV and realized that fifty years ago she knew both my mother and father—which was true. I remembered hearing her name.

She wrote, "Your father was a very handsome man. I saw you on TV . . . and you look like your mother."

3. One of the nicest compliments an author receives is to be asked to autograph a book. However, it becomes torture when you know the person but can't recall his or her name. Naturally, the person comes up to the desk and says, "Just inscribe it to me."

4. TV shows swallow up material faster than a black hole. On one show I was scheduled to appear before the snakes and after the chimpanzees. Also, on a TV show in Long Beach, California, two women appeared just before me selling franchises for a new type of in-home party. The products they were offering were flimsy negligees, garter belts, G-strings, lotions, body oils, and what they called "other apparatus." A tough act to follow.

5. Appearing on TV also broadens your knowledge about the broadcast medium. For example, you've probably heard TV hosts talk about having their guests wait in the "Green Room" before appearing on stage. I asked a TV producer why they called it the Green Room. His answer was: "That's because before they appear some guests turn that color and then get sick." (Note: Scholars speculate that the term "green room" originated in Shakespearean times when the "scene room" was where actors prepared to go on stage.)

6. A publicity tour also teaches you other show business sayings. For example, do you know why performers say to one another "break a leg" instead of "good luck" before going on stage? That, too, comes from Shakespearean times and refers to the act of bowing. When you bow to an audience, you bend (or break) your knee. So the well-wisher is hoping that you will earn bows after your performance.

7. One tour took me to southern California where I was booked in the famous Beverly Wilshire Hotel in Beverly Hills. When I reached my room, I found a large basket of fruit and a bottle of champagne awaiting me. "I guess I've reached semi-celebrity status," I concluded. The next

morning, when I left my room and walked down the hallway, I saw maids delivering fruit and champagne to *every* room. At the Beverly Wilshire, it appears everyone has celebrity status.

8. Speaking of celebrities, on one occasion, when I was booked on NBC's *Today Show,* I took my celebrity-struck daughter along to see the show in person. She was hoping she'd see people like Garth Brooks or Robin Williams. Instead, the guests that morning were heavyweight boxer Larry Holmes and a professional wrestler named "The Animal from Hell."

9. To learn the inside dope on celebrity status, talk to the limousine drivers. I was once booked as the luncheon speaker for 2,000 managers of Best Western Hotels. Captain James Lovell, hero of *Apollo 13,* was the morning speaker. He was absolutely wonderful. After my luncheon speech, the limo chauffeur was driving me to the airport and asked, "Did you hear Captain Lovell this morning?" I assured him I had. The driver said, "Yeah. A real hero. He even gave me a signed copy of his book. And then after I dropped him off at the airport I picked up Fran Tarkington. Great pro football player. National Football Hall of Fame . . . he's the speaker this afternoon. He's also written a book. He gave me a copy." Then, looking quizzically through the rearview mirror, the driver asked, "What do you do?" I explained that I had been the luncheon speaker. He said, "What do you speak about?" I explained that I talked about international business, protocol, etiquette, gestures, and things like that. After a pause, I added, "I've written a book, too. Would you like a copy?" He shook his head, and said, "Nah. I'm not interested in that international crap."

10. Finally, here is an actual letter I received after a book tour:

Dear Mr. Axtell,

I just read your book on hosting international visitors and I wonder if you can help me with a problem. I would like to be introduced to a nice Japanese businessman. Even an address would help. You see, I have 350 acres of timberland in Canada that I want to sell. Thanking you in advance.

Yours truly,
(Name)
Escondido, California

People often ask me, "As an author, what do you fear the most? Is it rejection? Or is it writer's block?" I respond that neither of those troubles me. Then I explain that I do have one great fear, and that fear is *garage sales*. (We call them "rummage sales" in our part of the country; in others they are called "yard sales"—but whatever they are called they're equally frightening.) They all seem to take the same form: a group of card tables in a garage or driveway, sometimes spilling over on to the grass, with each table displaying pure *junk*. My wife is a great "rummager," and on a few occasions she asks me to accompany her. I have, but with great trepidation. On one of those occasions I was wandering among the tables and—sure enough!—there was one of my books. My *newest* book! If you've ever visited one of these sales, you are acquainted with how items are priced—usually just for a dollar or dimes or quarters. So as I wandered past my book, I peeked at the price tag. Twenty-five cents! Then I noted that that figure had been crossed out, and "10 cents" was written underneath. Curious, and a bit upset, I sought out the woman conducting the yard sale and, without identifying myself, I asked, "I'm interested in that book, but what's wrong with it? Why is it marked down from 25 cents to 10 cents?" She replied very easily, "Oh, there's some *writing* in it." She opened the cover page and showed me: *I had autographed the book!*

Funny Stories from the Global Platform

For over almost thirty years, I have been a part-time evangelist for exporting—specifically, for encouraging more American companies to take up the business of exporting their product or their service. As explained in Chapter 8, the Department of Commerce claims that many companies in the United States are not exporting because of fear of the unknown. Managers of those companies complain: "I don't know how I'd get paid—I don't want *pesos* or *deutsche marks* or other 'funny money' like that. Furthermore, I don't know how to ship products overseas; I don't know about insurance, customs brokers, and duties. And, besides, I don't speak any other languages."

The solutions to all of those alleged obstacles are easy to provide, but the best way to convince people to export is to point to other companies, some selling uncommon products, that have become highly successful in exporting. And "successful" means "more profits" and "more growth." As a result, the following has become a standard part of one of my presentations on exporting:

> It has been proven repeatedly that companies that export grow faster and profit more than companies that do not export. And almost every type of product and service is exportable. For example, from my own home state, Wisconsin, we have companies selling bows and arrows to Japan, pool cues to Europe, and—if you believe it—even *chopsticks* to Japan, Taiwan, and Hong Kong. (The reason, incidentally, is the abundance of forests in Wisconsin; thus wood products are cheap.) We are also selling Christmas trees to Mexico and honey to Asia. Moreover, Wisconsin is America's largest exporter of ginseng to the Far East. Other companies are selling beer to Germany, perfume to France, and chicken feet to Hong Kong. *There is even a company in Ohio selling sand to Saudi Arabia!* Can you believe it? Sand to Saudi Arabia! The reason is the sand from Ohio is high in silicon, which is necessary to make glass, and the sand in Saudi Arabia does not have that ingredient.
>
> (I then save the best for last.) Listen to this. I recently heard of a company in South Carolina that is selling *cockroaches* to Mexico—they are used for laboratory experiments there.

When I revealed this last fact to one audience, a fellow in the back row blurted out: "My God! I've got a bonanza in my basement, and I didn't even know it!"

✝

In the winter months in North America, a massive migration occurs starting in the Canadian provinces down through the northern states, picking up wave after wave of usually older people. The eastern half of this mass seems to head for Florida, and the western half for places like Arizona and Nevada. Those popular tourist destinations often bear a love/hate relationship between the local residents and their visitors. Phoenix, Arizona, is one of those destinations. In the months of January through March, the population in metropolitan Phoenix almost doubles. For many years, the local residents labeled those visitors "Snowbirds." Eventually, that term seemed to acquire a tainted meaning, and so the local authorities tried to change the designation to the more benign term "winter visitors." However, if you talk candidly with some of the locals, you'll find they have fashioned their own special terminology. For example, many of the elderly types, when driving their autos with out-of-state license plates, are referred to as "cue tips." That is, of course, because of the appearance of all those white-topped heads barely peeking up over the level of the steering wheels. And if a bald-headed man happens to be driving, he is, of course, referred to as a "thumb."

✝

Humorous miscommunications occur in all societies, including our own. At my speaking engagements, I am often asked, "How did you get into this business of writing books and speaking about international protocol, etiquette, and communication?"

The following true story answers at least part of that question: I joined The Parker Pen Company in 1956 in the public relations department. In PR we are supposed to be professional communicators. One of my first assignments was to have the local newspaper, the *Janesville Daily Gazette*, report on a major top management change at Parker. There was—and still is—only one newspaper in Janesville, Wisconsin, which, incidentally, is where Parker was founded in 1888. My news story named the three executives who were taking over the management at Parker, and my task was to publicize this event as a major step forward, with promise and optimism for the future. On the appointed day, the editors of the paper printed my story. It contained just the right "spin," as we would call it today. Photographs of the three executives appeared in one vertical column, one photo atop the other, and my story was wrapped around the three pictures. When I saw all my material had been included in the news story, I concluded that I would probably have a long and good career with Parker. However, purely by accident, on that same day and on the same front page, there was another story, and it happened to be positioned *directly beneath the three photographs.* Unfortunately, since it was positioned directly under the three photos of the three executives, it seemed to be related to the three photos. The headline on that story read: THREE ARRESTED IN PIG THEFTS.

Shortly thereafter, I was transferred *out* of the public relations department. In fact, I was sent overseas, where I continued to make goofs and gaffes. But being an erstwhile journalist, I kept notes. And that led to writing books about protocol, etiquette, and proper communication. So now my motto in life is, "Into Each Life Some Pig Thefts Must Fall."

✝

Most of my international business counterparts were very adept businesspeople—intelligent, clever, and always good salespeople. One of the most memorable of them is the Parker distributor for all of Italy. His name is Giuseppe Fantacci. "Beppe," as he is called, was one of those extraordinary salespeople who was always smooth, persuasive, and articulate. For example, one of his favorite philosophies was "Never act your age." He and his wife, Marjorie, had eight children, and it became their custom that as each boy in the family reached a certain age, Beppe would take the son aside to explain the sensitive subject of "the facts of life." On one of those occasions it was time for the fourth son, Marco, to learn about this important passage in life. Beppe decided to take the boy on a fishing trip—just the two of them—so that they could spend a day establishing a good father/son relationship.

Later, Beppe reported that the day started out beautifully—gorgeous weather, smooth waters, and good fishing. He said, "I was able to gently edge into the subject of women and sex and then continue to the essential parts of marriage, love, conception, hygiene, and all the rest. I could see that Marco was listening intently. I knew I had his complete attention, so I explained everything—absolutely everything. Finally, after this lengthy monologue, I finished and said, 'Now, Marco . . . do you have any questions?'"

Marco replied, "Yes, Daddy. I do." There was a long pause, and then Marco asked: "How soon can I start?"

Later, as Beppe recounted this story to me, he added somewhat ruefully, "I think I may have oversold him."

+

Stewart S. was an American, born in Cuba and educated in Texas, who later became manager of the Parker Pen factory in Mexico. His elderly mother-in-law, "Mrs. M.," took up residence in a nursing home in the Parker headquarters city, Janesville, Wisconsin. Stewart, who was rather short and a bit overweight and an avid Texan, would visit her whenever he returned to the home office on business. Even though his mother-in-law's memory was almost entirely gone, Stewart was a dutiful son-in-law and visited her at the nursing home whenever possible. On one of these visits, he asked me to accompany him. In the process I overheard this conversation:

STEWART: Hello, Mrs. M. How are you today?

MRS. M.: Fine. But who are you? I don't seem to remember you.

STEWART: Oh, I'm just a friend of your family.

MRS. M.: Where are you from?

STEWART: Well, I'm originally from Texas.

MRS. M.: Oh, that's nice. My daughter married a man from Texas. Short little fat fellow. I never did like him.

✝

A third grade teacher in California once told me that she did a segment for her class about Europe and, specifically, about the different languages spoken there. Afterward, one youngster approached her, obviously troubled, and said, "I understand about those other languages, but English is the *real* language, isn't it?" She asked what he meant by "the real language." He said, "I mean, when babies are born they all speak English, don't they?"

✝

Almost every book has a page near the front consisting of a dedication. Most of the sentiments contained in those dedications are short, esoteric, and largely skipped over by the reader. However, occasionally they can provide an amusing anecdote. For example, I once wrote a book on public speaking. It was intended to help businesspeople improve their speaking skills. When writing the book, I sought help from an extremely talented business speaker in my company. His name is Arthur W. Foster. During the 1950s, Art spent many years traveling across the country conducting sales training classes for department store salesclerks in every state. As a result, he became especially competent at speechmaking and he built a wonderful repertoire of stories. At the company's quarterly sales meetings he was also always the headliner because he was so adept at both entertaining and motivating the sales force. In fact, at each meeting, the salespeople would become impatient until Art took the stage. As a result, it was natural for me to turn to Art for help in writing a book on business public speaking. Since he assisted me so significantly, I decided it would be appropriate to dedicate the book to him. I didn't mention this in advance because I wanted it to be a surprise.

When I received the first set of page proofs of the book, I sent the thick stack to Art with a short note simply asking him to review each segment to be sure I had faithfully reported his experiences and advice. Actually, I wanted him to discover the dedication himself. A week went by. Then another. And then a third. Finally, worried that I had seriously erred in the manuscript or had offended him in some way, I phoned him: "Art, did you get the manuscript?" "Oh, yes," he replied. "Well . . . ?" I asked. "What do you think?" He paused and then said very simply, "I don't know yet. I still haven't gotten past the dedication."

Postscript: I later found out that Art had been purposely waiting for me to phone him . . . *so he could use that line.* He is, indeed, the consummate speechmaker.

☨

When you conduct business internationally, one of the first rules you learn is to avoid getting involved in politics. However, after spending years respecting that taboo, veteran international businesspeople can be forgiven for taking good-natured potshots at the sacred territory of politics. For example, the following set of definitions for various forms of government is a popular source of amusement among international business travelers:

Communism: You have two cows. The government takes both of them and gives you part of the milk.

Socialism: You have two cows. The government takes one and gives it to your neighbor.

Fascism: You have two cows. The government takes both cows and sells you the milk.

Nazism: You have two cows. The government takes both your cows and then shoots you.

Bureaucracy: You have two cows. The government takes both of them, shoots one, milks the other, then pours the milk down the drain.

Capitalism: You have two cows. You sell one of them and buy a bull.

What happens in a democracy?

Democracy: Everyone has two cows. A vote is taken and the loser cries discrimination, the lawyers sue (on a contingency basis), and the government takes at least 39 percent.

✝

When I first began appearing on the speaking circuit, I was booked to speak to the annual meeting of the Wisconsin Cast Metals Association. The audience consisted of about a hundred executives associated with the foundry industry in my state. Along with the president of the association and the master of ceremonies, I was seated on a dais, which was raised about three feet off the floor, waiting to be introduced. Finally, I heard the words, "And now, here is our speaker for this morning, Roger Axtell." I buttoned my coat, pushed my chair back . . . and fell head-over-heels backward off the stage. Later, I was told I looked like Greg Louganis, the Olympic diver, dressed in a gray business suit. I could hear the audience both laugh and gasp. Someone rushed to my assistance. (I later concluded it's impossible to become injured in a fall like that because you're too darned embarrassed!) I brushed myself off, proceeded to the lectern accompanied by considerable laughter, and somehow began my remarks. Later that day, while driving home, I realized what I *should* have said in my opening. I decided a true professional speaker would have simply stood before the audience, smiled, brushed off some imaginary dust, and said: "Well, how do you like me so far?!"

✝

If you are ever called upon to make a speech, deliver a classroom lecture, or present a lengthy proposal to your board of directors, here is a bit of advice offered to me by a professional speechmaker. It deals with how much information an audience will retain in relation to the length of your speech. The formula passed along to me was as follows.

According to research, if you speak for ten minutes the audience will very likely remember your name, the title of your presentation, and two of the three most important points. If, however, you speak for twenty minutes, it is likely the audience will remember your name but not the title of your talk, and will remember only one of your three most important points. Finally, if you speak for fifty minutes, surveys show the audience will not remember your name, will not remember the title, and will have difficulty remembering even one of your most important points. In fact, the research indicated that during that fifty minutes some 68 percent would have spent the majority of your speech enjoying a silent sexual fantasy.

After I related this information to a large group of salespeople, a fellow in the back row shouted out, "Yeah! Go ahead! Speak for an hour!"

✝

And so we come to the end of this assortment of goofs, gaffes, faux pas, misunderstandings, and misstatements from the global village. This compilation is the result of thirty years of collecting and recording my own experiences plus systematically saving amusing news clippings, magazine columns, and letters from around the world. Many of the anecdotes in this book were hastily recorded on dinner napkins, matchbooks, business cards, or name tags after some world travel warrior related them to me.

There are over 300 stories in this book—some of them quite lengthy, and others just one-liners. I hope one or two of them generated a smile or even a chuckle. As I said in the introduction, the smile is the single best-known form of communication wherever you may travel. I hope you do it often.

Postscript

You may have noticed at the beginning of this book that it is dedicated to my father, Albert E. Axtell. Now I'll tell you why.

I wrote the following essay, which appeared in the Sunday magazine supplement of the *Milwaukee Journal* on Father's Day 1988:

> My father helps me warm up audiences. He's not there in person, mind you. It's my relating some of his one-liners that gets them chuckling.
>
> After-dinner speaking around the country is a part-time profession for me. As every speaker knows, it's essential to first get the audience relaxed and smiling. So I tell them about my father, Albert.
>
> He's ninety-three years old, I explain, and lives in Colorado. I say that when I attended his ninetieth birthday celebration, I turned to Dad and said, "I'm very proud of you, your great strength and integrity. To what do you owe your longevity?"
>
> He thought for a moment and, with the inborn timing of Victor Borge, replied, "I haven't had a glass of water in twenty years."
>
> Undaunted, I continued my talk with him.
>
> "Well, this is a special year for my wife and me, too. We're celebrating our thirty-third wedding anniversary."
>
> Dad paused for a few seconds, then said, "I had two of those."
>
> They've never set eyes on my father, but when I relate this dialogue, audiences love him. Often, in the question-and-answer sessions after my talks on international business, someone will shout, "Tell us more about your father!"
>
> More laughs. But then, for just an instant, I want to blurt

out, "I can't! Frankly, he's not cracking those jokes anymore. Right now he's sitting in a wheelchair in a veterans' home in Rifle, Colorado, confused, angry, and pleading with everyone that he needs money."

"I haven't got a dime in my pocket," he tells me on the phone.

That's untrue, of course. He has money. For starters, he has several $20 bills tucked in a round fabric-covered box in his drawer. And he has regular income from two pensions, plus some savings.

Besides, he doesn't need money, anyway. What would he do with it? He's propped in a wheelchair, legally blind, unable to hear unless you shout, and he slumps to one side from a stroke. Yet in his now fogged and humorless mind, some phantom fear roams, probably born of the Great Depression when "having a few bucks in your pocket" was the difference between dignity and dejection. And so he thinks he needs money.

Not long ago the quips and punch lines were still there. We'd go for walks around the block, him shuffling with that inching motion of Tim Conway.

He'd look up with a grin and say, "When people walk along with me, they have to adjust their stride a bit. On the other hand, when you throw me a pass, you don't have to lead me by much."

He was an infantryman in World War I, an amateur boxer and, between wars, a cavalryman. He was recalled to Army duty in World War II and rose from captain to colonel. His stride was different then.

Even when he was two blocks away, I could pick out his proud marching posture.

But the years slowed that gait and slanted that form. Still, the humor didn't leave him. In his eighties, he managed an apartment building occupied mainly by elderly women. On his monthly rounds of rent collecting, he would wear a baseball cap imprinted "Drop Your Bloomers." The women loved it.

He told me about one tenant who prayed daily to die. "Yet every day," he said, "she ate a banana, took her vitamins, and exercised. I told her I thought she was sending the Lord mixed signals."

"What's my outlook on the future?" he'd say. "Hell, I don't even buy green bananas." (His material was not always original. I'd heard that one before.)

He used to carry a small notebook around with him cataloging jokes to share with anyone who was in the mood. That book became famous and his sidekicks bantered about who would be lucky enough to be willed it when Dad died.

He didn't need his little black book, though, when I phoned him two years ago to announce proudly that, as a result of a book I'd written, I was booked to be interviewed on NBC's *Today Show*. "What the hell is that?" he asked. I told him to watch.

After I appeared on the show, I rushed back to the hotel and phoned him. "Well . . . how'd I do?"

With a trace of surprise in his voice, he said, "Better than I expected."

I persisted. "Well, other than that, Dad . . . how did I look on national television?"

"You looked old," he said.

My audiences like that line. They know instinctively that he was just keeping my feet on the ground.

As his eyesight and bearing diminished, they were replaced by frustration and irritability. My brother and I bought him a handheld tape recorder.

"Record your life," we urged. "You fought in two wars, your cavalry days alone are like Jack London adventure stories, and we want our children and their children to enjoy them as we have."

He liked that. For several months, he labored over his memoirs until one day he phoned me, upset.

"What's wrong?" I asked.

"Well, I want to do these recordings right," he answered. "I want to tell my life right from the beginning, in logical order. But I find myself getting the wars mixed up."

"Don't worry about that, Dad," I said. "No one can possibly relate his life's story with perfect chronology. Just talk into the machine. I'll edit the tapes later."

That familiar timing and smile returned to his voice: "Well, now that you put it that way, I don't even have to tell the truth, do I?"

People in my audiences will often ask me, "Did your father really say those things?"

I reply, "Yes. They're true. He said them."

But inwardly and silently I think, "But he won't anymore. It's gone. Now he only says, 'I haven't got a dime. I need money.' Now he thinks he's living with his sister. Now he asks if I've finished college yet. And I stand there in front of an audience, feeling guilty because I am lying, saying, 'Yes. He still says those great lines.'"

I don't have the courage to tell people the truth, that he dribbles his food, stares blankly ahead, and those cute young nurses have to reach into his food-filled mouth to remove his false teeth.

I often think, "What am I going to do when he dies? Can I continue the myth? Will I keep telling the same warm-up stories about my father? Can I pretend to myself and my audiences that he's still out there snapping off those wisecracks and one-liners?"

My answer is yes. I'll lie and pretend. I'll do it, and the reason is simple. It's because that's the way I want to remember him, and him to be remembered.

Just as the smell of a cigar brings him back into a room with me, a good laugh erases that image of a helpless man complaining that he doesn't have a dime.

And, when I hear the laughter I see only his incomparable smile, and above it that baseball cap with the words "Drop Your Bloomers."

After this article appeared, I sent a copy to the nurses at the Veterans Administration nursing home in Colorado, and within a week or so, I received the following letter from one of the nurses:

Dear Roger,

We received the wonderful article about your father. I read parts of it to him, and I think he understood and enjoyed it.

He has his good days and his bad days. On his good days he's as sharp as ever. I went in to see him the other day and even though he seemed alert, I could see that he was having a bad day and was depressed, so I said, "What's wrong, Albert? Having a bad day?"

He replied "Yes, I'm tired of this life. I can't read or watch TV. I ache all over. I can't sleep well. To be perfectly frank, I'd just as soon end it all . . . *check out*, any day now."

I told him it was OK to think that way. That surprised him, and he said, "Really? Is it OK to think that way?" I reminded him that he'd had a good, long life and much to be thankful for.

He said, "Well, it's true I've had a *long* life . . . but to be truthful, I wasn't exactly *good* all that time."

I asked what he meant by that, and he said, "Well, in my day, to be perfectly frank, I was known as something of a womanizer."

So I said that was OK, too. Again he looked surprised and said, "You really think that was OK?" And when I repeated, "Yes . . . it's OK," he grinned at me with that wonderful smile of his and said, "Well . . . if it's OK . . . *why don't you hop in bed with me?*"

One year later, on July 9, 1989, my father passed away. And since then, I've kept my word. I've tried to keep his memory alive. As I promised in the *Milwaukee Journal* essay, every time I stand before an audience I pretend that he's still cracking those jokes and one-liners. For each of these appearances, to assist the person who must introduce me, I have fashioned a rather unconventional introduction. Rather than have the presenter read all the customary credentials about college degrees, honors, publications, and number and names of children, I provide the following text:

(Introduction for Roger E. Axtell)

It is now my pleasure to introduce our speaker, Roger Axtell. On occasions like this, I think it is important to do some research. So, when I learned that Roger's ninety-four-year-old father, Albert Axtell, lived in Glenwood Springs, Colorado, I decided to write him and ask for information about his son. Here is the reply I received:

Dear _____ ,

You wrote requesting information about my son, Roger. Here it is.

How would you like to be:

- An adviser to three Wisconsin governors
- A speaker in demand around the country
- And a tournament-ranked tennis player?

Well . . . so would Roger!

Instead, Roger worked thirty years for the Parker Pen Company until his retirement a few years ago. His last job was as vice president, Worldwide Marketing. He lived and traveled abroad for Parker for twenty-five of those years. As a result, he has written seven books on international business, protocol, travel, hosting, communicating, and even gestures and body language.

His books have been translated into as many as eleven different languages.

He is also a frequent guest on national TV talk shows. He's appeared on NBC's *Today Show,* the *Regis Philbin Show,* the *Merv Griffin Show,* CNN's *International Hour,* and both British and Canadian national television. ABC's *Good Morning America* has invited him to appear on six separate occasions.

He was also once booked on the *David Letterman Show* but was bumped at the last minute by a dancing-dog act.

It's true that he has worked for three Wisconsin governors and served the current governor Tommy Thompson for eight years as a special assistant for business. He did this for a dollar a year, which makes me wonder about his business sense, and explains why I have his older brother handle all my financial affairs.

I hope he does a good job at your meeting. He needs the experience. The first time he appeared before an audience was in the fourth grade, when he portrayed Davy Crockett . . . and he wet his pants right on stage!

Signed: Albert E. Axtell

With that introduction from his own father . . . here is our speaker, Roger Axtell.

And that is why this book of humor is dedicated to my father.

Index